Contents

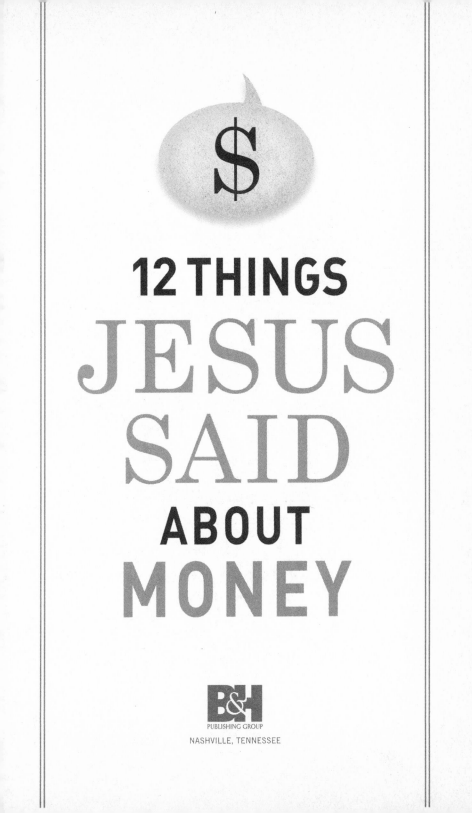

12 THINGS
JESUS
SAID
ABOUT
MONEY

B&H
PUBLISHING GROUP

NASHVILLE, TENNESSEE

978-1-4336-4568-6

Published by B&H Publishing Group
Nashville, Tennessee

Dewey Classification: 248.6
Subject Heading: PERSONAL FINANCE
\ STEWARDSHIP \ MONEY

1 2 3 4 5 6 7 8 • 21 20 19 18 17 16

Introduction

You may not think of Jesus as a good financial counselor. Good counselor, yes. But financial counselor? Money advisor? Outside of *giving* money, which He seems to want us to do a lot of, what else did He really tell us about it?

Well, quite a lot actually is the right answer. And while you won't automatically turn into a financial whiz by working your way through these few pages, you might just discover the kind of wisdom that could significantly impact more levels of your financial life than you realize.

Each chapter looks at a specific theme, connecting various teachings of Jesus into a readable, shareable, teachable experience. While ideal as a chapter-a-day devotional, you might also find it suitable as a weekly discussion starter to share with your spouse or family and kids, or for a small Bible study group or class. Several open-ended questions have been added after each chapter for personalizing and further discussion.

Plus, if you desire to go deeper on your own into what Jesus said, all the verses that appear in every chapter are listed separately at the end by reference. You might consider spending some more in-depth moments with the Lord by reading through and meditating on these Scriptures at another time, to see what else He can show you.

Because Jesus simply has so much to say . . .

And hearing Him say it can truly change everything.

Let's start with our money, and see where He takes us from there.

1

On Priorities

There's Only Room for One Number One

You cannot be slaves of God and of money. (Matthew 6:24)

Each day's carload of activities and priorities can only seat a twenty-four-hour assortment—not a second more—despite all our best time-saving methods, despite whatever amount of multitasking we do to try maximizing the space. But according to Jesus, our main problem is not that we're trying to do too much (although, of course, we certainly may be). Our biggest problem in this area is not as closely tied to what's *riding around* with us as to what's *driving* us.

Many can ride. But only one can drive.

Or to put it in Jesus' words, "No one can be a slave of two masters" (Matt. 6:24). Because as long as there's competition for the driver's seat, there will always be conflicting opinions over which passengers we allow to fill up our available scheduling blocks—what stays and what goes, for how long and for how far. As long as there's more than one driver, we'll struggle to be consistent in how we determine where everything's supposed to go and how it's all supposed to fit together.

And *that's* why the resulting chaos is so often such a mess.

Too many drivers, like too many cooks, is a stock recipe for burnout.

And so here's where the discussion, as it often does, spins back around to money . . . because while our choice of possible driving candidates can number in the dozens, Jesus singled out one of them for special mention—*money*—arguably the most bossy, demanding, and lead-footed driver of them all. Not just money, but the craving to make more money. To impress other people with money. To regularly lose sleep over money. To satisfy our various aches and itches with money. To mask our underlying, unspoken needs with money. To steer our kids toward whatever might generate the most scholarship money.

Money. Always something to do with money.

When money is doing the driving, you're much more inclined to think of it as the best answer to whatever problem or question you may be facing. When money is doing the driving, you're much *less* inclined to see other things—lasting things, investing-in-people-and-relationship things—as being the most valuable use of your time right now. And that's the kind of thinking that puts second- and third-best priorities at the top of each day's passenger list.

Because, yes, you may often resonate with a lot of what money is telling you. But the biblical fact is that "you cannot be slaves of God and of money." You'll need to pick one.

Because you can't have both.

Not to say, now, that you can't be a Christian and simultaneously be influenced by financial considerations of any kind. Money is a gift from God, a legitimate means of trade and basic survival. Jesus (we'll see as we go along) said too much about money for us to interpret Christian living in purely monkish, idealistic terms—a detached, out-there existence that pretends money doesn't even matter. *Sure,* it does. You need it. And He knows it.

But having it, and earning it, and using it, and investing it are not the same as being *driven* by it. Money is not the real issue here. The issue is: *What's driving you?* Because we *cannot* . . . *will* not . . . *must* not be slave-driven by money.

The only driver suitable for us is the same one that drove Jesus—His Father in heaven—like when He stood up to Satan's temptations by quoting Scriptures that said, "Man must not live on bread alone but on every word that comes from the mouth of God" (Matt. 4:4). "Worship the Lord your God and serve Him only" (Luke 4:8). "I do not do seek My own will," He later said to those who challenged His authority. The only "will" that Jesus followed was "the will of Him who sent Me" (John 5:30).

God and God alone must occupy our driver's seat . . . because that's the only way we're going anywhere successfully.

Chasing the Impossible

The sticking point here, of course, is that we don't really believe that. We don't tend to equate Him with some of the measures of success we've always had in mind. Dig deep enough into most of our hearts, and you'll see we're not actually too comfortable with God being our exclusive driver. We're not convinced that sitting completely under His control is a good way, definitely not a *sure* way, of moving forward in a way that's truly, financially best for us. More likely, we think, if we let Him have total charge of things, He'll guilt us into sending our money to some remote mission outpost in the wilds of Africa—or, heaven help us, maybe even send us there ourselves. And *then* what will become of our career path, our dream house, our children's college options, our retirement fund projections? He obviously hasn't been reading the pie charts and percentage-savings goals we've been getting from the Charles Schwab people lately.

No, but the truth is, there's an eternity's worth of confidence behind Jesus' invitation to "come to Me, all of you who are weary and burdened" by all these worries and concerns about doing enough and having enough, "and I will give you rest" (Matt. 11:28). "Whoever does the will of My Father in heaven," He said, "that person is My brother and sister and mother" (12:50). That's the person—in other words, the one who lets God do all the driving—who'll experience the deepest, most intimate, most behind-the-scenes enjoyment of life with Him, as opposed to those who are foolish enough to think that money—ha, money!—can ever come anywhere close to providing what up-close fellowship with Christ can offer.

Money, let's admit, simply by the look of things, does appear to be a good driver. We've seen, for instance, the gated communities and three-car garages where it's capable of taking people—and not just the filthy rich, but even some of those really nice, really humble, really generous people at church who sure seem to have the whole package working for them. Pretty sweet, it seems. But money, if you'll watch it carefully over time, typically does more *chasing* than *driving*. It's always after the next thing, the next deal, the next growth strategy, the next investment opportunity. It keeps us desperate both to get ahead and stay ahead, at whatever cost these objectives demand. And while the goal behind going for them may be quite well-meaning, even quite well-placed, the chase can become all-consuming—all too slavery inducing—until we're feverishly, obsessively running hard after things that actually, upon closer inspection, are probably best just to walk away from.

Because "what is a man benefitted if he gains the whole world, yet loses or forfeits himself?" (Luke 9:25). "For whoever wants to save his life"—by making sure there's ample money to support his desired lifestyle—"will lose it," Jesus said. "But whoever loses his life because of Me will find it" (Matt. 16:25)—by trusting that our good and loving Creator is undoubtedly much better than we are at knowing how to maximize a believer's full potential.

Still sounds sort of risky, though, doesn't it? Losing what feels secure in order to find what really matters? But this is only a risk to those who are arrogant enough to think they know something God doesn't. It's only a risk to those who think they have something of their own—in their money or at least in their big plans for making money—that He can't quite match with anything of His.

One and Done

Jesus was being accused of having a demon inside of Him when He made the following statement, but it applies nicely to this whole matter of loyalties, allegiances, and priorities. "Every kingdom divided against itself is headed for destruction, and a house divided against itself falls" (Luke 11:17). The idea that we can have our God moments, mixed in with our greedy moments, mixed in with a lot of other not-so-God-inspired moments, and still expect to come out whole on the other end is a real mistake in logic.

Our hearts, in order to function at their best, were made for beating at a steady pace. At *one* pace. And if we hope to capably incorporate all our necessary priorities—even occasionally just some desirable priorities—into this swinging dance of life, we must understand they will only stay in rhythm with each other if the overall cadence is being set by the pulse of God's tempo. There's simply no way that any other arrangement can work in our lives. Not and be happy with the music it makes.

In fact, even the things you'd expect to receive God's automatic seal of approval as regular fill-in drivers will actually prove problematic if you let them push Him out of His number one leadership position. Jesus said in Matthew 10:37, "The person who loves father or mother more than Me is not worthy of Me." *What?! My own parents?* "The person who loves son or daughter more than Me is not worthy of Me." *What?! My own children?* "Yes, and even his own life," He added in Luke 14:26. *What?! My own health and diet and exercise and everything?!*

Okay, we know from our own gut, as well as from the Scriptures themselves: *Parents?* Huge priority. They're right there in the Ten Commandments. *Children?* Huge priority. "Let the little children come to Me," Jesus said, "because the kingdom of God belongs to such as these" (Luke 18:16). *Care for our own lives and well-being?* Huge priority. If the second greatest commandment is to "love your neighbor as yourself" (Mark 12:31), then loving self is obviously expected to function at a high benchmark in our lives.

But there's a reason why these major, legitimate priorities ride underneath the *first* greatest commandment—which is to "love the Lord your God with all your heart, with all your soul, with all your mind, and with all your strength" (Mark 12:30) . . . because when *that* priority is established and lived by, that's how all these other important passengers on our priority list (yes, including our money) receive the absolute best part of us that we can bring to them.

Seriously, no one besides God—not even our family and kids—can be counted on as a reliable driver. And knowing this, why would we ever think of money as the one exception?

So we shouldn't get so shaken up when Jesus says, "Every one of you who does not say good-bye to all his possessions cannot be My disciple" (Luke 14:33). It's not because He wants us foraging for nuts, berries, and firewood in the forest. It's not because the only righteous bank account is the one with a daily balance of zero. But until we get clear on the following two truths—(1) that God is actually the owner of everything and (2) that He actually does delight in giving "good things to those who ask Him" (Matt. 7:11)—we will keep clutching our money with a death grip, claiming it as our own, refusing to turn it over. Then, instead of watching Him transform it into a tool of blessing and fulfillment in our hands, we'll see it continuing to eat up precious space on our priority list, while continually eating away at our sense of contentment, freedom, pure worship, and joy.

There's a good chance, even this very day, you've been trying to do too much. Your calendar is likely bulging at the margins, with maybe a good half-dozen things to try to accomplish or finish up before you go to bed tonight. What's more, thoughts of money may be top-of-mind on your concerns right now, whether from job troubles or car repairs or any number of household matters that—Christian or not—still require cash on hand in order to pay for them.

But if you'll put your faith in what Jesus has said, deciding against all fear and worry and hungry ambition that you are going to choose *one* Master to drive you—and one Master only—you will find at some mile-marker along the journey that, hey, this life of yours is starting to feel a lot more confident and complete. A lot less motivated by money. And even with a ton of things to handle and manage and figure out and referee, at least you know that God, your now-permanent driver, has already been down this road before. And while most of the other cars in traffic are veering out of control (the way *your* car used to do), yours is now under trusted navigation and leadership.

Turns out that driving with two hands on the wheel isn't the safest method after all. Best to drive with one hand—as long as that "one hand" belongs to Him.

For Family and Bible Study Discussion

1. Where would you say money ranks on your overall list of priorities? What comes above it?
2. In what ways have you experienced the feeling of being a "slave" of money?
3. What are the real barriers between *you* and total allegiance to God? Why do you think you keep them there, or at least really struggle to remove them?
4. What role or place *should* money occupy in your heart, in your thinking, in how you prioritize each day?

Words of Jesus from this chapter—Matt. 4:4; Matt. 6:24; Matt. 7:11; Matt. 10:37; Matt. 11:28; Matt. 12:50; Matt. 16:25; Mark 12:30–31; Luke 4:8; Luke 9:25; Luke 11:17; Luke 14:26; Luke 14:33; Luke 18:16; John 5:30

2

On Contentment

Today's Supply Is Enough for Today

Give us each day our daily bread. (Luke 11:3)

Teach us to pray," Jesus' disciples asked Him (Luke 11:1). They'd often seen Him retreat into quiet, deserted places, sometimes very early in the morning, spending precious hours in prayer, which, in all honesty, they probably thought could have been put to better use. The crowds, after all, were pressing hard every minute to see Him, to experience Him, to get from Him what He alone seemed able to offer them. Couldn't He maybe cut His prayer time a little shorter? Free up some more hours in His schedule? Take full advantage of this popular platform He was growing?

Yet what they saw in Him—the intensity, the authority, the astonishing power, the tender compassion . . . maybe whatever He was receiving from His Father in prayer was worth the cost in diminished opportunities for exposure and appearances.

And so they deemed it worth asking Him: "Lord, teach us to pray." Their request indicates a sense of wonder and curiosity. What was He saying and doing in prayer that made Him able to say and do what they observed in Him every single day? More personally, what could *they* be saying and doing in prayer that could give them just a little bit of what He obviously had?

All of us want to know, then as now: What can we do to be more like Jesus?

One of the answers, which comes down to us from the teaching He gave them—captured within the passage now known as the Model Prayer or the Lord's Prayer—is this simple-hearted statement of dependency on the Father for each day's provision:

"Give us today our daily bread" (Matt. 6:11).

Help us be satisfied, Lord, with each day's supply, knowing that *You* know it will always be enough for whatever we need.

The biblical term for this godly character trait is *contentment*—like when Paul, warning about the corrupting, enslaving possibilities of money, told the young pastor Timothy that "godliness with contentment is a great gain" (1 Tim. 6:6). Paul reminded him how we came into this world with nothing. How we will leave this world with nothing. And how as long as we have "food and clothing"—the basic, everyday necessities of life—the presence of *contentment* in our hearts will be of far more value to us than whatever else could be added financially to our sum total (vv. 7–8).

Jesus, naturally, is our perfect model for this. Among the qualities that apparently kept Him inspired and at peace on the earth was His complete contentment with the life His Father had given Him. He was able to be satisfied with "food to eat" that others didn't even know about (John 4:32). "My food," He said, "is to do the will of Him who sent Me and to finish His work" (v. 34). Being content with the Father's choice of gifts—materially and otherwise—kept Him resting in the joys of another world, even while the struggles of *this* world played out all around Him.

Contentment for those in relationship with Christ is a powerful, nearly impenetrable asset to possess. Those who have it—you can't really rattle them. Their desires are few. Their threshold of need is low. Their faith is completely in God. And as long as they've got His promise of "daily bread" to fall back on . . . you know what? They're good.

What a strong place to live, huh?

And it's where Jesus says *we* can live. Every day.

What a Difference a Day Makes

Throughout Scripture, God places a great deal of importance on the measurement of time we commonly know as a *day*, as well as on our present-tense awareness of the day— *this* day, today—that we've been given the privilege of living.

The account of Creation, of course, is marked off in days. "Evening came and then morning . . . and God saw that it was good" (Gen. 1:8, 12). The writer of Hebrews instructed believers to "encourage each other daily, while it is still called today" (3:13), not putting off the right-now opportunities for growth and impact that are readily available to be experienced between now and nightfall. The writer of Psalm 95, in a passage that hearkened back to the children of Israel's experience in the wilderness, challenged his readers to listen for God's voice "today," and not to "harden your hearts" like earlier generations who refused to be satisfied with what the Lord had provided them (vv. 7–8). After all, "You don't even know what tomorrow will bring," said James, the brother of Jesus, in the Bible book bearing his name, "for you are like smoke that appears for a little while, then vanishes" (James 4:14).

Today is really the only day we ought to be concerned about.

So let's think about that for a second. Isn't it caring of God to compress our lives down into these series of days, into these easily conceived units of time? We take this regular twenty-four-hour pattern for absolute granted. It's so baked into our infrastructure, we rarely stop to consider He could've opted to arrange our concept of time in any other way He wanted. Yet in His gracious understanding of our human needs and natures, He chose to provide us with these fresh, new, sunrise beginnings that roll around with such remarkable frequency, we sometimes look up and wonder where the day (or the week, or the whole summer) has gone.

But there's a lot more blessing contained within these routine rhythms of life than we realize. We're people who, with such a limited sense of perspective, cannot really process the full span of our lives in one screenshot. Can't wrap our brains all the way around it. We *can*, however—and God knows it—fairly easily grasp the distance between waking up today and waking up tomorrow. *That* much we can figure.

And for *that* long, Jesus said, we can stay content inside.

He knows we could never bulk up our contentment muscles enough to be able to support our full weight from now till the end of our lives without strain, without a hitch, without a depressing, exhausting sense of breakdown. But with Him feeding and clothing and providing for us day by day, maybe we actually *can* make it from now till bedtime without complaining or feeling sorry for ourselves or caving in to hopelessness over our financial situation.

"Therefore don't worry about tomorrow," Jesus tells us, "because tomorrow will worry about itself" (Matt. 6:34). And by that time, His faithful mercies will be "new every morning" all over again (Lam. 3:23) so that we can crank our contentment meter back up, running strong with a whole new, fresh set of batteries.

Contentment—whether in terms of money or anything else—is truly a daily experience.

Comprehensive Coverage

"This is why I tell you," Jesus said, "don't worry about your life, what you will eat or what you will drink; or about your body, what you will wear. Isn't life more than food and the body more than clothing?" (Matt. 6:25).

Easy for Him to say, right?—"don't worry"—when, listen, we can look around and see all kinds of things to be worried about. But this "don't worry" advice is much easier to accept when we realize the true immensity of the One who's saying it. And so Jesus, in trying to calm down these understandable concerns about our everyday, material needs, gave us two reasons why we can take Him to the bank on it.

1. *If He can do greater things, surely He can do lesser things.* Jesus and His capabilities represent ultimate greatness. "Apart

from Him not one thing was created that has been created" (John 1:3)—not a single dot-sized organism or dust speck. "Life was in Him," John the apostle told us, "and that life was the light of men" (v. 4). The only reason any of us are sitting here today is because of the creative power and grace of Almighty God.

Here's the financial spin on that. Why, having put so much divine investment into giving us life, into fashioning our bodies, into knowing us inside and out, down to the molecular level and beyond—physically, emotionally, mentally, spiritually—why would He suddenly stop short at the last second and not make sure He equips these creations of His with everything we need? Why would He prove Himself able to do something so mind-blowing as speaking us into existence from absolute nothingness, and then prove somehow unable to keep us afloat enough to survive? Makes no sense, right?

But, okay, if that argument doesn't seem solid enough for you, Jesus also came at it from the other direction.

2. *If He does lesser things, why wouldn't He also do greater things?* "Look at the birds of the sky: They don't sow or reap or gather into barns, yet your heavenly Father feeds them. Aren't you worth much more than they?" (Matt. 6:26). Or, "Learn how the wildflowers of the field grow: they don't labor or spin thread. Yet I tell you that not even Solomon in all his splendor"—long considered the richest king in Israel's history—"was adorned like one of these" (vv. 28–29).

Not one of the birds or beetles or buttercups outside your window today is sweating its future or fretting the change of weather. The animate ones (the birds, for example) are out there doing their daily work, living the way God intended them, while the vegetative ones (the "wildflowers" in Jesus' illustration) are just standing there with their leaves and blooms pointed beautifully toward the heavens. And if God is carefully tending to the daily needs of such relatively insignificant creatures within their small-world context of being, why has He decided to cut off this same (and greater) level of need meeting when it comes to us human beings, the crown of His creation?

Or as Jesus more succinctly put it, "If that's how God clothes the grass of the field, which is here today and thrown into the furnace tomorrow, won't He do much more for you?" (v. 30).

Bottom line: "your heavenly Father knows" what you need (v. 32). And since He is the One who meets every need of every description throughout the universe, His promise of "daily bread" is all the confidence you need, too, for staying content each day with your circumstances, whatever those may be.

Our tendency, of course, is to not be quite satisfied with these circumstances. Because, no kidding, they can truly press us to the wall sometimes. And God, since He is good and caring and willing to respond to the cries of our heart, welcomes us to approach Him continually in prayer, asking for what seems to be lacking in our pocketbooks and pantries.

But the opposite of contentment—and here's where the real problem comes in—is not just this passive sense of *dis*contentment. It actually goes a lot deeper, and a lot darker. Discontentment leads to worry, which can lead toward a rather chronic case of self-pity, which can then lead to anger, then to bitterness, then to hardness of heart, relational breakdown, and from there on to misery. Discontentment will ultimately take us to places that none of us really want to go.

That's why the heart He wants to grow within us is one that is satisfied and unworried with the current status of the day. Not that His teaching precludes believers from gaining wealth—in fact, as we'll see, He expects fruit production and the multiplying of resources—but He knows contentment will always serve us best in whatever situation we find ourselves.

Some believe the lessons of Matthew 6:25–34 are a continuation of what the writer of Proverbs 30 taught, when he set to words this prayer to God: "Give me neither poverty nor wealth; feed me with the food I need. Otherwise, I might have too much and deny you, saying 'Who is the LORD?' or I might have nothing and steal, profaning the name of my God" (vv. 8–9).

Jesus, we know, is fully capable of taking five loaves and two fish and feeding five thousand men with the miraculous proceeds, ending up with twelve baskets of uneaten scraps left over (Matt. 14:19–21). But perhaps even more incredible—and more pertinent to keeping our relationship with Him close and trusting—is how He can take the five loaves and two fish in our take-home pay, and spread it sufficiently enough throughout our spiritual system that we can lie down at night *content* with being completely in our Savior's care.

For Family and Bible Study Discussion

1. Name someone you'd identify as a truly contented person, someone who's modeled this trait in various life circumstances. What helps make them that way?

2. How could having a consistent one-day focus impact your life, particularly in terms of how you handle and think of money?

3. Think of other examples from nature (in addition to birds and wildflowers) where God's complete provision, wisdom, and forethought are clearly on display?

4. Where would you expect a life of chronic discontentment to lead?

Words of Jesus from this chapter—Matt. 6:25–34; Luke 11:1–3; John 4:32–34

3

On Faith

Appearance of Lack Gives Opportunity for Belief

Keep asking, and it will be given to you. (Luke 11:9)

C losely related to the importance of *contentment* is the imperative of *faith*. The two of them travel as sort of a pack. They are the interlocking gears that roll us forward onto the battlefield of each day, coming together to make us nearly impervious to any situation . . . armed with *faith* in a God whose abundance is beyond calculation, and *contentment* with a God who is sufficient for our every need.

Hard to find a chink in that armor.

But faith is worth separating out for its own specific look, since faith not only is the ground upon which we enter into saving relationship with Jesus Christ (Gal. 3:11), but is also intended to be our onboard navigation system for all of life. "We walk by faith, not by sight," Paul reminded us (2 Cor. 5:7). And this same principle applies in our approach to money as it does to everything else.

Okay now. Start talking about *faith* and *money* in the same sentence, and our antennas immediately go up. We start to detect the visual images of tacky hairdos, tailored suits, and the overhyped promises of televangelist appeals. But if any of us choose to get hung up there, throwing the baby out with the prepackaged holy water, we'll miss the actual truth of what Jesus said on the subject. So flush the bad taste out of your system, if it's there. Reach for a big glass of biblical truth to rinse with. And do not disqualify your financial portfolio, nor your financial need, from the effects of faith on its value and potential.

Our money, like every other gift from God we've been entrusted to steward, is meant to be a vehicle through which He operates, working through our faith to create fresh evidence of His power and glory in our lives. It's not about us. It's not even about the money. It's about the all-wise, all-loving, superior will of God responding to faith where He sees it, then using our faith as an opening to accomplish new scenes of testimony through us.

Jesus, for example, told the story of a widow who was being unjustly treated. He didn't specify what had been done to her, but we can imagine it was an injury or inequity that was affecting her livelihood, her security, and her already precarious standing as a widow in the culture of that day. But whatever it was, financial or otherwise, here's what she did about it: she kept going in person to one of the town officials—"a judge," Jesus called him—repeating the same appeal, again and again, "Give me justice against my adversary." And though the hardened man tried every rude way in the world to dismiss the woman and refuse her request, she eventually—"because this widow keeps pestering me"—couldn't be denied. "I will give her justice," the exasperated judge said, "so she doesn't wear me out by her persistent coming" (Luke 18:1–5). She finally got what she came for.

Now God, of course, unlike the judge in this story, is not a rolling-his-eyes, get-out-of-my-face-lady kind of authority figure in our lives. But Jesus said if even a man who was inclined to keep telling this widow no—in no uncertain terms—could finally succumb to her faithful determination, "will not God grant justice to His elect who cry out to Him day and night? Will He delay to help them?" Absolutely not. "He will swiftly grant them justice. Nevertheless," He added, "when the Son of Man comes, will He find that faith on earth?" (vv. 6–8). Will He find us looking to Him with that kind of bold resolve and expectation?

Earlier Jesus had told a similar story. A person went to his neighbor at midnight, having been surprised at a late hour by unexpected company, caught without enough food in the house to offer his guest a meal. "Friend," he said to his neighbor, "lend me three loaves of bread." And then probably added a "please" at the end. *You don't mind, do you?*

Well, apparently he did mind. "Don't bother me!" came back the answer. "The door is already locked, and my children and I have gone to bed. I can't get up to give you anything." *Go home and leave me alone!* But Jesus said, "Even though he won't get up and give him anything because he is his friend, yet because of his friend's persistence"—there's that word again—"he will get up and give him as much as he needs" (Luke 11:5–8).

Now let's assume Jesus expects us to try placing ourselves directly into this scenario. So imagine for a moment that you're the unprepared host in this story. Your guest is hungry and tired from a long day's traveling. You're upset with what little you have to offer, but you feel sure your neighbor probably has enough to share. And obviously—you'll be sure to tell your neighbor this, the minute you see him—you'll pay him back first thing tomorrow once the stores open. Even double the amount.

But it's late. You feel bad about bothering him. It's an awkward situation, all the way around. Yet after weighing your unpleasant alternatives, you decide to go ahead and do it. You knot up your courage and walk next door, tapping ever so softly to keep from jarring the whole house awake.

And then—the thing you were most worried about—you get this angry, irritated response in return.

What next, then? Get angry back? Yell and point fingers? Raise your voice level to match his? Tell him to never expect you to come to his aid either the next time he wants something similar from you?

Or would you more likely be the mousy type—backing away in apology, sorry you disturbed him, kicking yourself for thinking you had a right to impose, wishing you could just crawl in a hole right now?

Based on Jesus' final teaching point of the parable, the reaction we're left to envision is quite different from either of these majority positions. Instead, we get the impression the person stood right there in that doorway, weathered the knee-jerk frustration of his neighbor, and continued to respectfully but passionately—persistently—plead his case for why he needed this bread at this hour.

And that's what your God wants to see from you, too, as Jesus tells it. *Persistence.* No quit. Not taking the first no as final. Showing up again in the morning, and the next day, and the next day after that—still "asking," still "searching," still "knocking" (Luke 11:9).

By faith.

Persistently Parental

"*Keep* asking," in fact, is what He really said. "Keep asking." "Keep searching." "Keep knocking." That's because the best answer to every question—the best possible response to any need—is whatever you receive from the loving, caring hand of your heavenly Father. For though other streams of resource and support may be available or seem more immediately reliable—and while His answer to your prayer may lead you to any of those places—the important thing is that you're looking to Him for direction first. He is your beginning point. And midpoint. And endpoint. And all points.

Start there.

And stay there.

And prepare to be met with provision there.

That's because *He* is your answer, even more than the answer is.

It's what happened with the Canaanite mother in Matthew 15 who came to Jesus asking for healing for her daughter. His first response, His second response—both responses tested her desire to keep pursuing Him, to believe in His willingness and ability to help. But she'd become convinced, having probably tried everything else, that even the crumbs of His blessing—as long as they were coming from Jesus—would be more desirable than the best result of her own bootstrap efforts. "Woman, your faith is great," He answered her. "Let it be done for you as you want" (v. 28).

The rationale Jesus gave in Luke 11 for our "keep asking" assurance of faith is this: God's identity toward you as Father. Which, depending on your life history, may or may not arrive as a welcome relief. Some of us haven't been trained by past experience to expect the role of a father in our lives to be a good and kind one. Maybe one of those people is you. Perhaps longtime patterns of abuse have broken your trust that anything but harm or betrayal is what you're most likely to receive from a father. Perhaps the indifferent neglect you've experienced has caused you to think you wouldn't deserve God's kind attention even if He were somehow inclined to give it to you. And while, yes, our common heritage as sinners makes each of us unworthy recipients of His generous help, the depth of His genuine love and mercy toward us as His children causes Him to want to bless us with the full balance of what we need.

"What father among you," Jesus posed to His original listeners, "if his son asks for a fish, will give him a snake instead of a fish? Or if he asks for an egg, will give him a scorpion?" (Luke 11:11–12). Again, your answer to questions like these, which sound so rhetorical to some, may be, "Well, *I* can sure think of one"—and you've got the emotional snakes-and-scorpions scars to prove it. But the focus here isn't on *your* father. The focus is on *God* the Father, whose faithful, responsible nature is exactly what Jesus, His own Son, reports it to be. He is the giver of "good gifts" (v. 13); the deliverer of good things.

So the faith you place in Him to meet you at your point of need is not blind faith, not wishful faith, not superstitious faith, not hope-I've-been-good-enough-lately faith that might somehow, barely have a shot at overriding His rejection of your request. No, it is *trusting faith*—the kind that confidently concludes, as Jesus taught us, "All the things you pray and ask for—believe that you have received them, and you will have them" (Mark 11:24). Or if not that, something even better.

The way a perfect Father would do it.

Pursuing the Pursuer

You know your own reasons for why faith comes hard for you—as it typically does for all of us. Maybe it's an inborn independent streak. You don't like asking for help from *anybody*. Maybe it's risk avoidance, a layer of protection you carefully apply to your heart that keeps you from ever getting your hopes up—better than being let down by another disappointment. Perhaps for other people it's laziness. Or spiritual disinterest. Or self-absorption. Or whatever.

But if you tend to find the action of faith too pushy or too needy—all this "keep asking, keep searching, keep knocking" and everything—realize these are actually the same kinds of actions Jesus models for us Himself. Remember His story of the man who had a hundred sheep (Luke 15:3–7) but who found out that one of them had wandered off? Remember His story of the woman who had ten coins (vv. 8–10) but who was counting them one day and could only find nine?

The shepherd who won't stop until the lost sheep is cradled around his shoulders . . . the person who sweeps the whole house until that single missing coin is found . . . the one who stands at the door and knocks, saying, "If anyone hears My voice and opens the door, I will come in to him and have dinner with him, and he with Me" (Rev. 3:20).

That's what Jesus did and keeps doing for you. He's the One who keeps coming and won't quit, who keeps knocking expecting an answer. The part of faith that feels like you're chasing Him down, being pesky and annoying, interrupting His schedule and all—the reason it doesn't feel that way to Him is because He's actually the One pursuing you. And your heart.

And, yes, above all—His glory.

Which leads to the one question we all need to answer ourselves: Is glory what He'll get from us by meeting and exceeding our financial needs?

If so, then bring them before Him, same as all your other needs. Because "whatever you ask in My name," He said, "I will do it so that the Father may be glorified in the Son" (John 14:13). How He chooses to be glorified in you, of course, will be unique to your situation and in sync with His perfect sense of timing. Faith is not a plug-in program that generates a fixed order of results. But "if you remain in Me," Jesus said, "and My words remain in you"—if you *keep* seeking Him, as much as you're seeking His answers—"ask whatever you want and it will be done for you" (15:7).

Have faith. In Him. For everything.

And keep it up.

For Family and Bible Study Discussion

1. What are some inspiring examples of faith you've seen in others or in your own family?
2. Why might God require persistence on our part, even in prayer? Why shouldn't He just give us stuff?
3. What current financial need or situation in your life could be fertile ground for planting a deeper measure of faith?
4. How would you describe the tension or relationship between faith and contentment?

Words of Jesus from this chapter—Matt. 15:28; Mark 11:24; Luke 11:5–13; Luke 15:1–10; Luke 18:1–8; John 14:13; John 15:7

4

On Humility

Place a High Value on Simple Things

The Son of Man did not come to be served,
but to serve. (Matthew 20:28)

We'd never do it, of course. It's so impractical, we'd consider it absurd even thinking about, but . . .

How would you feel about somebody who literally, willingly, radically just took a complete vow of poverty—no longer laid claim to any money or possessions, swore off all forms of material good, survived on the most meager resources possible—all with a desire for living in pure, unencumbered devotion to God.

Maybe you'd think they were crazy, sure. That'd be one easy conclusion to draw. But if you happened to see them out somewhere—happy, contented, relaxed, trusting, unworried, unhurried, seemingly at total peace with themselves, able to spend long hours at what they love, genuinely caring and serving and taking time for others—wouldn't you have to say they possessed something spiritually special that the rest of us

. . . just kind of don't? Wouldn't you be likely to consider them closer to God's heart than perhaps you currently are?

The things Jesus said about money, let's be clear, do not leave us restricted to this one kind of expression toward it. To austere lifestyles. To the rigorous deconstruction of our financial houses. He's created us too unique, too distinct, to be thinly drawn in the form of a single model—all of us the same, all across the board. He warned us, in fact, not to judge each other "according to outward appearances" (John 7:24). Of *any* kind. He said that righteousness is no more found in giving things away (Matt. 6:1) than in piling them up (23:5–7). The "pure in heart" (5:8)—the ones He said will "see God," the ones who will stand forever in the presence of His glory—aren't made that way by how much money they make or don't make. Our faith in Him, our faithful life with Him, is not defined by measurements of decimal points and dollar signs, by either their presence or their absence.

But while poverty, within itself, is no more holy than wealth, there are certain characteristics that do seem to emanate more naturally from a needy heart than from any other. And they're the kinds of things we each need to seek and desire.

One of them is the awareness of being "poor in spirit" (Matt. 5:3). Money, we know, tends to give off a seductive air of self-funded security. Its five- and six-digit numbers have a way of coming together to form a much softer mattress and pillow to sleep on. With sufficient funds in our various spending and saving accounts, we're likely to view ourselves as adequately prepared for the common eventualities of life—ones that for other people, less moneyed people, can still roar loudly enough in the distance to worry them half to death.

But money, if not seen for what it is, can tempt us into giving it far more credit than it's due. It can leap the boundaries where it rightfully exists as a commodity of fair trade for goods and services, and pretend it's also capable of contributing to our spiritual success, spiritual strength, spiritual resilience, and spiritual standing as well. Money can place a mask on us that hides a key aspect of ourselves from being nearly as exposed to our eyes as it needs to be.

"The kingdom of heaven," Jesus said, belongs to these "poor in spirit"—those who refuse to be tricked, by money or anything else, into overlooking the spiritual bankruptcy that lives within their hearts, just as it lives within the heart of every person. Because without this ongoing awareness of need, we'll walk our polished shoes past important areas of repentance every day—places where, if we were in better touch with reality, we'd be looking into the puddles around our feet, and seeing the reflection of a man or woman who is hardly the sum of our carefully imaged parts.

Becoming poor in spirit is not only a wise *life* plan but, oddly enough, also a wise *financial* plan.

As is "hunger" and "thirst" (Matt. 5:6). Again, money is good at disguising things, at being able to coddle us with temporary satisfaction of our temporary desires, and thereby keeps us from experiencing the wow, the joy that results from having our *deepest* desires met instead.

"Those who hunger and thirst for righteousness," Jesus said, "are blessed." Big-time.

Let's cash this out a little bit. Those who think more about their next life (with Christ, in heaven) than their next meal (with choice of yummy sides) will find something that sticks to their ribs and their soul a whole lot longer. Those who crave seeing Christ's character taking the place of those stubborn pockets of sin in their lives can have a big thanksgiving dinner every day of the week, even on days when Thanksgiving is still weeks and months away. Such people are "filled" with the love of Jesus, and "filled" with the confidence that their salvation is indeed a reality. A prize they can actually live with. Like, right now.

And, no, you don't need to be penniless to experience these poor, hungry, thirsty requirements for being blessed, filled, and gratified in the truest of ways. But you cannot allow money to shield you from realizing your need for them. And you cannot live as though you're financially exempt from stooping down to deal with them.

Keys to Greatness

The place where these changes in perspective can take us is to *humility*. Which is a beautiful, beautiful thing. Cannot put a price tag on its value. But what's funny about humility is that it's not really a destination. It's not something you check off once you get there. You actually just kind of absorb it along the way. It grows in the background, while you're off trying to let Jesus be Lord instead of you.

And even when you've got it—even when humility is breaking out all over you—you're typically the last one to see it. In fact, you'll *never* see it. Because if you see it, if you start to notice it, if you begin to recognize how humble you're becoming, that's actually just a dead ringer for telling you, "Hey—you don't really have it."

This is not to say humility is something that just happens. Humility is part of what God breeds in our hearts within a steady, sustained process of change, but . . . well, when you're clearing away the stuff that keeps you from being poor in spirit, when you're hungering and thirsting for righteousness, when (like Jesus) you're seeking to serve rather than to be served—yeah, humility *does* just sort of happen.

And wouldn't you love if it happened to you?

Because, guess what—humility is actually the doorway to greatness.

Jesus made this clear in a parable that showed the striking contrast between the folly of pride and the honor of humility. Two men, He said, came into the temple to pray—one a Pharisee (from among the largest group of Jewish leaders in Jesus' day) and the other a tax collector (considered the scum of the earth, stereotypically notorious for their ill-gotten gain).

"The Pharisee took his stand and was praying like this: 'God, I thank You that I'm not like other people—greedy, unrighteous, adulterers, or even like this tax collector. I fast twice a week; I give a tenth of everything I get'" (Luke 18:11–12). Pretty impressed with himself, you might say—and certainly assured that God was mighty impressed as well.

"But the tax collector, standing far off, would not even raise his eyes to heaven but kept striking his chest and saying, 'God, turn Your wrath from me—a sinner!'" (v. 13).

"I tell you," Jesus summed it up, "this one"—this tax collector—"went down to his house justified rather than the other." Then pay special attention to His next phrase. "Because everyone who exalts himself will be humbled, but the one who humbles himself will be exalted" (v. 14).

There you go. One of the most oft-repeated themes in Jesus' teaching.

"You know that the rulers of the Gentiles dominate them, and the men of high position exercise power over them. It must not be like that among you. On the contrary, whoever wants to become great among you must be your servant, and whoever wants to be first among you must be your slave" (Matt. 20:25–27)

Say it again. "When you are invited by someone to a wedding banquet, don't recline at the best place . . . go and recline in the lowest place." Not with an artificial show of humility, but because that's truly how you see yourself, as owing all your importance to what Christ has done by redeeming a sinner like you, like all of us. "For everyone who exalts himself will be humbled, and the one who humbles himself will be exalted" (Luke 14:8, 11).

Again. "Unless you are converted and become like children, you will never enter the kingdom of heaven. Therefore, whoever humbles himself like this child," Jesus said, pointing to a youngster He'd invited to come stand with Him, "this one is the greatest in the kingdom of heaven" (Matt. 18:3–4).

The humble don't need to be made a fuss over. Don't need to be burdened about how they're coming across. Don't need to keep their head on a swivel hoping to be noticed. Don't need to be sure everyone can see how well they've done in life.

They can live instead a much simpler life—not easier, but simpler—by putting others first, looking to serve, feeling released from padding their own résumés, and being satisfied with who they are in Christ, not in what they've achieved and what they've obviously got to show for it.

Simplify

In Matthew 10, as Jesus dispatched His disciples on their first ministry assignment, He sent them out with a few simple instructions. Among His directions were these: "Don't take along gold, silver, or copper for your money-belts. Don't take a traveling bag for the road, or an extra shirt, sandals, or a walking stick" (vv. 9–10). And on and on like that.

The importance of these verses for us today is not in the details. In fact, the Bible mentions another time when Jesus told them, yes, "whoever has a money-bag should take it, and also a traveling bag. And whoever doesn't have a sword should sell his robe and buy one" (Luke 22:36). So obviously, we don't need to get legalistically tangled up in the weeds on this. But here's what we *do* need to tie on to: Let's understand that God will always be faithful to supply our needs. Let's travel light without hoarding and storing away extras of everything—the kind of extras that will likely just end up getting thrown out later anyhow. Let's focus more today on who we're representing than on what we look like and how well everything's laundered, labeled, and coordinated. Let's make the kingdom of God, not the kingdom of self, the reason why we head out into the world tomorrow.

Because great things (God things) can happen when we do.

Seems pretty clear by now that Jesus isn't calling us to some kind of minimalist, barebones, monochromatic existence. That's not what He has in mind for His followers. As long as we're solidly under His leadership—doing whatever He says to do—He basically gives us freedom of movement up and down the financial spectrum.

But here's what else should be clear: our hearts are easily polluted and pulled away from total devotion to Christ. It doesn't take much to distract us and create distance. So while you needn't feel automatically guilty for having exorbitantly more net worth than the poorest of the poor in the world, you might still do well—for your humble heart's sake—in seeking to simplify your current holdings, hobbies, and personal habits.

Do you really need another sport jacket, for example? Twenty pairs of shoes? Will it kill you not to get a new hunting bow this season? Couldn't you probably make do with the telephone and television you already own? Don't you already have enough stuff to insure and pay monthly bills for the privilege of accessing? If acquiring wasn't on your mind so much, wouldn't you be freed up to think about other things? More helpful things? More holy things? More simple yet satisfying things?

Humility doesn't restrict you to minimum-wage earnings or to an old beater in the driveway that leaks oil like a crop duster. But nothing is worth having, no matter how nice and comfortable, if it's bought in exchange for a heart that inflates its self-importance, forgets what it's really made of, and confuses greatness with ownership.

Keep it simple. Or you'll be sorry.

For Family and Bible Study Discussion

1. Create your own working definition of what being "poor in spirit" means. Why would Jesus call it a "blessed" or "happy" attribute to have?
2. What works the hardest against your humility?
3. What have you learned from your own or others' experiences with having a shortage of money?
4. Where could you simplify your lifestyle and give yourself some increased financial freedom?

Words of Jesus from this chapter—Matt. 5:3; Matt. 5:6; Matt. 6:1; Matt. 10:9–10; Matt. 18:3–4; Matt. 20:25–28; Matt. 23:5–7; Luke 14:8, 11; Luke 18:11–14; Luke 22:36; John 7:24

5

On Wealth

Money Will Always Want More from You

The worries of this age and the seduction of wealth choke the word. (Matthew 13:22)

Watch out and be on guard against all greed," Jesus said to a crowd of thousands one day, "because one's life is not in the abundance of his possessions" (Luke 12:15). And once we've heard this statement of principle from Him, perhaps that's all we really need to know on the subject of wealth and financial attainment.

Watch out, you guys. Be careful.

And don't lose sight of what life's all about.

Because it sure isn't money. Or anything money can buy.

And yet we've been fed an opposite line for so long—by implication and osmosis, if not exactly by direct quote—we probably need to allow more time than this for the idea to sink all the way down into our hearts. Because money, we've sure been led to believe, could fix a whole lot of what's wrong with us and our lives, if only we had more of it.

No, *that's* what's wrong.

Wrong primarily because of a particular truth that gives us the hardest time believing. Not intellectually perhaps, but we just can't seem to live and think as though it's true. It's what David attempted to encapsulate by saying that "every mortal man is only a vapor" (Ps. 39:5), "like a breath . . . like a passing shadow" (144:4), "like grass . . . like a flower of the field; when the wind passes over it, it vanishes, and its place is no longer known" (103:15–16).

This life, in other words, from the perspective of eternity, is something like the following living room conversation:

"Did anybody hear that?"

"Hear what?"

"Outside. That noise, like a . . . I don't know, like a . . ."

"Nope. I didn't hear anything."

"I could've sworn I . . . You're sure you didn't hear it?"

"No." (All look at each other. All agree.) "No."

"Hmm. Maybe it was just the wind blowing or something."

"Yeah, probably nothing."

There and gone. Over and done. Like a dustup of wind blowing through. But believe it or not, that's what the Bible says our *whole lifetimes* are like. They sail by us that fast. Like a flicker of light on the wall, like a rustle we thought we heard through the back window, but now we don't hear it anymore, so . . . *(Forget I mentioned it, what were we talking about again?)* The grim, or actually beautiful, reality is that our lives are a flash of an instant, then we're suddenly at home with Jesus. And when we get there, then we'll fully understand just how brief it all was.

But *money* often prevents us from seeing it that way. Money, because of the focus and importance we feel compelled to give to it, magnifies out of all proportion this whisper of a moment, this brief window of earthly life that simply doesn't justify an overemphasis on things that only matter for a heartbeat. As David said again, "Certainly man walks about like a mere shadow. Indeed, they frantically rush around in vain, gathering possessions without knowing who will get them" (Ps. 39:6).

That's because money—unlike God, unlike our eternal souls, unlike even the personal friendships and relationships we develop with others—doesn't have a future beyond this wink of an eye we call a human lifetime. Money has a known use and role and necessity for the time being, but when that time is over, it's getting left in the dust, never to be heard from again. Utterly worthless. No matter how much of it we've made or amassed.

The attainment of wealth is a fine accomplishment. And there are many good reasons for doing so. But if we want to understand the place it needs to occupy in our lives, Jesus said we need to position it within the context of a life *w-a-a-a-y* more than just the small part of it that's visible from here on the earth.

Wrong-Track Minds

Jesus communicated this recalibration of mind-set in a couple of parables, one of them involving the contrast between a rich man who dressed in "purple and fine linen, feasting lavishly every day," and a poor man named Lazarus who "longed to be filled with what fell from the rich man's table" (Luke 16:19–21). Their lives came; their lives went. And though the poor man was "carried away by the angels to Abraham's side," the rich man found himself in torment, looking up and seeing Abraham "a long way off" (vv. 22–23).

"Son," Jesus said that Abraham said, "remember that during your life you received your good things, just as Lazarus received bad things, but now he is comforted here, while you are in agony" (v. 25). The cozy collateral of wealth had paid out as much as it could pay in the rich man's life, and now it couldn't even cover the cost of a single fingertip of water to cool his scalded tongue.

Money can only do so much. And can only do it for so long.

Perhaps more well known (and more telling) is Jesus' story of the wealthy farmer whose acreage had become so profitable and productive, he'd run out of room for housing the bounty of his annual yield. "What should I do," he thought to himself, "since I don't have anywhere to store my crops?" (Luke 12:16–17).

Maybe while waiting for him to answer his own question, we could think of some possible answers for him ourselves. As in, perhaps he could distribute some of his overabundance to the poor, to the hungry. Or establish a work-based cooperative that incentivized an employee's labor with the promise of food for their family. Or partner with another agricultural operation that could help him out with his storage problem in exchange for helping *them* out with income from his rental fees. Who knows?

But here's what we know he decided instead. "I'll tear down my barns and build bigger ones and store all my grain and my goods there" (v. 18).

In all fairness, now, there's nothing automatically wrong with that approach. Job creation. Opportunity expansion. Purchases of lumber and supplies that could benefit the local economy. But his business model was based on a spiritual model that couldn't support long-term success. And worse yet, it ended up earning his worldview a withering rebuke from Jesus. For in all his thinking, the man led himself to conclude, "You have many goods stored up for many years. Take it easy; eat, drink, and enjoy yourself." To which God responded, "You fool! This very night your life is demanded of you. And the things you have prepared—whose will they be?" (vv. 19–20).

Life is so short. So incredibly short. And "the one who stores up treasure for himself and is not rich toward God" is sure to find out in short order that the pursuit of wealth alone—without a corresponding wealth in long-term spiritual investments—is the shortest of shortsighted strategies (v. 21). Wealth, for all its apparent promise and payoff, is in the end a dangerous errand.

As Jesus continually warned . . .

The prodigal son, for example, desired early wealth through illegitimate entitlement rather than hardworking employment. But after squandering his father's premature inheritance with rapid selfishness and irresponsibility, he ended up wishing he could eat the soiled, fly-infested leavings that were slopped to the hogs for their daily consumption (Luke 15:11–16). Wealth alone, all by itself, had proven fleeting and foolish.

The rich young ruler apparently pursued wealth with the same methodical intensity with which he pursued legalistic purity and well-dressed self-righteousness. But when given a radical commission from Jesus that cut to the heart of where his true motivations lay, "he was stunned at this demand and he went away grieving, because he had many possessions" (Mark 10:17–22). Wealth had sent him chasing after the wrong goal, and even in hitting it, he still missed it.

The Pharisees, described by Luke as "lovers of money," scoffed at Jesus' teaching about the inferior priority of wealth, about its failure as a primary life ambition. "You are the ones who justify yourselves in the sight of others," Jesus told them, "but God knows your hearts. For what is highly admired by people"—whether it's wealth or whatever else is meant to measure one's status on the earth—"is revolting in God's sight" (Luke 16:14–15).

Time to cycle back here to Jesus' opening statement again: "Watch out and be on guard against all greed because one's life is not in the abundance of his possessions." Let's hope we're getting the message He strongly means to convey.

Credits and Debits

All right, if you're starting to feel the money leaking out of your back pocket . . . if you're feeling a bit guilty now for attaching that upcoming raise or bonus to the installation of new countertops in the kitchen—despite the fact that your current countertops are perfectly fine, even if slightly last-decade—prepare for a little bounce-back of spiritual permission.

Money is fine.

Having it and making it are good.

In fact, multiplication is desired and expected.

Think of the landowner in Jesus' parable who leased out his vineyard to tenant farmers. "When the grape harvest drew near, he sent his slaves to the farmers to collect his fruit" (Matt. 21:33–34). In a similar parable, a traveling nobleman came home to his servants to "find out how much they had made in business" (Luke 19:15). The man expected to see growth and production—and praised those who'd turned a profit on their initial investment. In fact, he chastised the one who *hadn't* grown his income. "Why didn't you put my money in the bank" at least? And then "when I returned, I would have collected it with interest!" (v. 23).

Listen, we have been "appointed" by Christ to "go out and produce fruit" (John 15:16). We're to be like the "good ground" that received the planting of God's Word and "produced a crop that increased 30, 60, and 100 times what was sown" (Mark 4:8). Now, certainly the theme of this instruction is spiritual in nature, not merely financial and material. But there's no reason to limit the biblical principles of faithfulness, hard work, and anticipated production to nonsecular purposes alone.

We've been created to grow, mature, produce, and develop—and equally, if not more seriously, cautioned against the opposite. When Jesus, hungry, approached a lone fig tree along the roadside "and found nothing on it except leaves," He vented His dissatisfaction by causing the tree to die . . . immediately (Matt. 21:19). When a vineyard worker and his employer came across a plant that hadn't borne fruit for three years, the master ordered, "Cut it down! Why should it even waste the soil?" (Luke 13:7).

"To everyone who has, more will be given," Jesus routinely taught, "and he will have more than enough. But from the one who does not have, even what he has will be taken away from him" (Matt. 25:29). The exemplary person in Jesus' eyes is the one whose boss, when he shows up to check on him, "finds him working" . . . for such a man "will be rewarded" (24:46). Industry, achievement, and its resulting wealth are nothing to apologize for. In fact, they are things we should consistently and nobly strive for.

And yet . . .

Never forget . . .

"Watch out and be on guard against all greed because one's life is not in the abundance of his possessions." Or as He said it another way: "How hard it is for those who have wealth to enter the kingdom of God! For it is easier for a camel to go through the eye of a needle than for a rich person to enter the kingdom of God" (Luke 18:24–25).

The problem, again, is not the money itself. The problem is what we allow money to become in our hearts. The problem is that our wealth—the pursuit of it, the growing of it, as well as the fretful, expensive protecting of it—keeps our heads down, our thoughts inward, and our vision all too limited to this tiny landing strip of earthly life.

Hear how Paul interpreted these truths of Jesus: "Instruct those who are rich in the present age not to be arrogant or to set their hope on the uncertainty of wealth, but on God, who richly provides us with all things to enjoy. Instruct them to do good, to be rich in good works, to be generous, willing to share, storing up for themselves a good reserve for the age to come"—not as a heavenly minded denial of wealth as a responsible goal, but "so that they may take hold of life that is real" (1 Tim. 6:17–19).

And definitely much longer lasting.

For Family and Bible Study Discussion

1. How many of your goals in life are financial in nature?
2. Why wouldn't Jesus just come out and declare wealth as being bad, evil, sinful?
3. How have you been influenced by greed, and what effect does it have on your relationship with God?
4. What kinds of bold changes could you make that would counter the temptation toward greed?

Words of Jesus from this chapter—Matt. 13:22; Matt. 21:19; Matt. 21:33–34; Matt. 24:46; Matt. 25:29; Mark 4:8; Luke 12:15–21; Luke 13:7; Luke 15:11–16; Luke 16:14–15; Luke 16:19–23; Luke 18:24–25; Luke 19:15; Luke 19:23; John 15:16

6

On Investing

Use Earthly Resources for Heavenly Purposes

*For where your treasure is, there your
heart will be also. (Matthew 6:21)*

Some of the mysterious paradoxes of Jesus' message were hard to grasp for the people who first heard Him speak, same as it remains to many today. He had come from God, He said. He was going to die, He said. But He was going to bring life, He said.

What did that mean exactly?

And yet "as He was saying these things, many believed in Him" (John 8:30). They looked around at what their experiences had left them, the darkness and hardness they felt. They took stock of what little they'd received from chasing after the endless rules and regulations of their religion, from springing to all the jump-higher demands of their leaders. Futility, hopelessness, pointlessness—these seemed to be the only return they could ever expect, not only from their compulsory adherence to such legalistic weights and measures, but also to the inner struggle they fought against the sin in their hearts, as well as against the strife and injustices that circled so wearingly around them every day. They wanted more. They wanted better. They wanted . . .

Freedom? Yes, freedom.

Freedom's a good word for it.

So they surely perked up at what Jesus said next: "If you continue in My word, you really are My disciples. You will know the truth, and the truth will"—get ready for it—"set you free" (vv. 31–32).

Jesus came to set us free.

When you read on in John 8, you meet a cast of (unbelieving) characters who were obviously defensive of the beliefs they already held. And they were defiantly opposed to anyone—especially this unlearned teacher—who dared refer to their brand of truth and teaching as slavery. But by the end of the chapter, there's no doubt who comes off looking like the confident authority and which ones are left appearing whiny, threatened, and desperate. A prideful heart and mind, chained in bondage to one's own self-serving arguments and opinions, is such an unbecoming picture, is it not?

But freedom, on the other hand.

Freedom looks and feels incredible.

Not only in Jesus, but also in His people.

Yet this "set you free" reality that Jesus has established in our hearts is not confined to Sunday worship service and other spiritual settings. It's also meant to feather out into every other extremity and engagement . . . until freedom is what we actually begin to experience in every single area of our lives.

Our money included.

But even though we do want the freedom of being released from money's grip and immediacy on our hearts and in our thoughts, we don't know if we can really afford it. We may not buck against it with the stiff know-it-all-ness of the Pharisees, but we're pretty sure God hasn't thought all the way around the implications of this freedom—what it means (for mere mortals like us) to live with such light cares about today and such unquestioning confidence in tomorrow. It's not that easy, you know?

And therefore we don't feel freedom very often.

But couldn't we? If we really believed? Believed the truth?

Between Doing and Being

Jesus and a group of His followers dropped in on some friends—a pair of sisters named Mary and Martha—while traveling through the village of Bethany, a couple of miles outside Jerusalem. Martha, apparently the more fussy and pragmatic of the two, began busying herself with the preparing of refreshments and accommodations for their guests. Good for her. Good old Martha. But Mary, in a move that must have struck her sister as somewhere between rude and irresponsible, didn't run to get one towel, or to make up one bed, or to sweep even one corner of the room. Instead, she just "sat at the Lord's feet . . . listening to what He said" (Luke 10:39), seemingly oblivious to everything else.

Humph. Fancy that. Little Miss Mary. Not lifting a finger. Just sitting there, while Martha dusted and cleaned up around her. You can imagine the extra bit of banging and clattering she was probably making, more loudly than the job required, sort of clearing her throat to get Jesus' attention, wordlessly cocking her head and eyes in Mary's direction. *Are You seeing this, Lord? I'm not getting much help here, if You hadn't noticed.* When the power of semi-subtle suggestion didn't seem to be achieving her desired effect, Martha finally blurted out: "Lord, don't You care that my sister has left me to serve alone? So tell her to give me a hand" (v. 40).

Wonder what kind of look Jesus shot her in response. We could probably call it kind and patient. Understanding and unbothered. He knew Martha, just like He knows us. He knew she'd feel lazy and antsy if she weren't scurrying around, picking up after people, doing the day's bidding and business. But "Martha," He said, surely behind a caring smile, wishing she knew what He meant, wishing she knew who He really was and what was really happening in her home that day. "Martha, Martha"—*oh, Martha, Martha*—"you are worried and upset about many things, but one thing is necessary. Mary has made the right choice, and it will not be taken away from her" (vv. 41–42).

Imagine now the look on *Martha's* face. "The right choice"? What Mary's doing here is the "right choice"? And mine, I guess, is the "wrong choice"?

No, Martha. Not the wrong choice. Just not the best choice. The choice to live in freedom. Not to "work for the food that perishes but for the food that lasts for eternal life" (John 6:27). Not to "collect for yourselves treasures on earth, where moth and rust destroy and where thieves break in and steal. But collect for yourselves treasures in heaven, where neither moth nor rust destroys, and where thieves don't break in and steal. For where your treasure is," Jesus said—whether it's imbalanced toward the earthly and temporary, or more trustingly tilted toward the heavenly and eternal—"there your heart will be also" (Matt. 6:19–21).

No, it's not *wrong* to invest ourselves so deeply here—in our money, our fortunes, our plans for advancing up the ladder of success and prosperity. It's just not *everything.* And it doesn't even compare to what we *could* be doing if we were continually investing the bulk of our time, resources, and money into eternally secure positions. Wherever Jesus would lead us to do it.

He came up against people all the time who said they believed Him and wanted to follow Him, those who were drawn to the freedom He was offering them. But when He invited them to step in further—not merely with a toe dip but with a cannonball into the deep end—He often got some hang-back, hold-up-a-second reactions in return. They're similar to those that appear in one of His parables, the one about a man who invited a bunch of people to a big banquet he was throwing. And yet one after another they answered with excuses like:

"I have bought a field, and I must go out and see it."

"I have bought five yoke of oxen, and I'm going to try them out."

"I just got married, and therefore I'm unable to come" (Luke 14:18–20).

Okay, fine. Go check out your field. Go play with your oxen. Go pretend that marriage somehow excludes you from serving Jesus with your whole heart. But look what happens when business and personal agendas and, yes, even the smokescreen of family obligations come between *you* and the opportunity for investing in the lasting commodities of Christ. As Jesus said, "What is a man benefited if he gains the whole world, yet loses or forfeits himself?" (Luke 9:25). "Anyone finding his life will lose it, and anyone losing his life because of Me will find it" (Matt. 10:39). As He said to the Pharisees who were so enamored with the temple and their influence in and around it, "Which is greater"—the "gold" of the temple itself "or the sanctuary that sanctified the gold" (23:17), the God who is more valuable than all the gold in all the temples in all the world put together?

To the woman He met at a Samaritan well, Jesus said, "Everyone who drinks from this water will get thirsty again. But whoever drinks from the water that I will give him will never get thirsty again—ever! In fact, the water I will give him will become a well of water springing up within him for eternal life" (John 4:13–14).

And if we really believed this—believed it as the truth— wouldn't we feel like we could invest in Him without risk, fear, or worry? With freedom?

The Sweet Smell of Surrender

Jesus was back through Bethany one day, visiting in the home of Simon, a Pharisee. They were eating dinner, likely engaging in some enlightening conversation, when a woman came up behind Him carrying a marbled, translucent jar of expensive, sweet-smelling perfume. It was Martha's sister Mary (you remember Mary) who "stood behind Him at His feet, weeping, and began to wash His feet with her tears. She wiped His feet with the hair of her head, kissing them and anointing them with the fragrant oil" (Luke 7:37–38). Takes a lot of freedom to do a thing like that.

Two men, two reactions to this provocative scene. The first was Simon, host of the dinner event, who wondered aloud what kind of woman just barges into a man's home like this, interrupting their meal with such an outlandish spectacle.

Jesus, however, used the rare opportunity to give Simon something else to wonder about. "Do you see this woman? I entered your house; you gave Me no water for My feet, but she, with her tears, has washed My feet and wiped them with her hair. You gave Me no kiss, but she hasn't stopped kissing My feet since I came in. You didn't anoint My head with olive oil, but she has anointed My feet with fragrant oil. Therefore I tell you, her many sins have been forgiven; that's why she loved much. But the one who is forgiven little, loves little" (vv. 44–47).

Forgiveness. Have we perhaps not grappled with the truth— the real truth—behind our sins? Behind our forgiveness? Are we aware of just how dead and depraved our hearts had been before Jesus chose, in such remarkable mercy, to throw out our whole putrid mess of it? And if we came closer to understanding the depths of this truth, would our freedom to invest in Him, instead of in ourselves and our immediate plans, be more natural, responsive, and extravagant?

A second reaction. From Judas. (Yes, that one. The one who would later betray Him.) "Why," Judas asked, incredulous at what he was seeing, "wasn't this fragrant oil sold for 300 denarii—an amount of money roughly equal to a full year's wages for a common worker—and given to the poor?" (John

12:5). John commented that Judas "didn't say this because he cared about the poor but because he was a thief. He was in charge of the money-bag and would steal part of what was put in it" (v. 6). So Jesus, knowing the heart behind the question, answered Judas by saying, "Leave her alone; she has kept it for the day of My burial. For you always have the poor with you, but you do not always have Me" (vv. 7–8).

Motive. Have we perhaps not grappled with the truth—the real truth—behind what drives our decisions and reactions? And if we could authentically clear out the selfish angles, the me-first, smartest-guy-in-the-room attitudes, as well as the two-faced pretensions that lead us to say one thing but mean another, would we not discover a freedom of motive that might just settle all the way down into what we did with our money?

Which of the participants in this event demonstrated a heart that was functioning in freedom? Simon the Pharisee, only half thinking he needed what Jesus could do for him? Judas Iscariot, whose conflicts of soul constantly fought against his allegiance to Christ? Or Mary, whose disregard for normal conventions and others' opinions, matched with a head-first love and loyalty toward Jesus, went all in with heavy investments of herself and her resources in giving God glory, in making Him her absolute first among all other rivals?

Each of us comes into every day carrying our finite assortment of things to invest. How free will you be today to put them into places where they'll still be paying dividends long after much lesser investments have been drained of all their potential?

For Family and Bible Study Discussion

1. What are some of the Martha-style obligations and expectations of yourself that consistently prevent you from enjoying Mary's style of freedom?
2. Thinking about some of the financial decisions you're currently or will soon be facing, what might make the difference between an okay choice and a best choice?
3. How might a lack of extreme gratitude to God affect how you handle your money?
4. What are some of the competing motives you often notice when making spending decisions?

Words of Jesus from this chapter—Matt. 6:19–21; Matt. 10:39; Matt. 23:17; Luke 7:44–47; Luke 9:25; Luke 10:41–42; Luke 14:18–20; John 4:13–14; John 6:27; John 8:31–32; John 12:7–8

7

On Greed

Turn the Tables on Indulgent Desires

*Stop turning My Father's house into
a marketplace! (John 2:16)*

I
n anyone's list of the most memorable scenes from Jesus'
earthly life and ministry, the account of His cleansing of
the temple would likely rank top ten in most of them—the
day He forcibly drove the moneychangers from the house of
God.

Like His miraculous feeding of the five thousand, this
moment proved indelible enough to be recorded by all four
of the Gospel writers. Maybe because it was so unexpected?
Maybe because it had been a silent wish of so many for so
long? Maybe because any man with this much steely courage,
unafraid of taking the fight directly against corruption and
injustice, could truly be the promised Messiah?

For us, perhaps, the main appeal of this story is probably
something else: the unabashed demonstration of righteous
anger. As being a *good* thing. Even a Jesus thing. Our world

has done a fairly thorough job of softening His image into a smooth-skinned, doe-eyed, harmless purveyor of peace and love. But seeing Him bullwhipping the fat cats of religiously sanctioned greed; upending the tables where they'd set up shop in the temple; backhanding their cash drawers into loud, spraying ricochets of scattered coins; and prodding loose their marketable inventory of doves, sheep, and oxen from the pens and cages of commerce . . .

Yeah! We love that!

The truth, of course, is that everything Jesus did throughout His time on the earth was an expression of otherworldly strength. The fact that He would tolerate even one word of derisive contempt from people who (whether they realized it or not) were only alive because He had personally created them— you talk about restraint. The difficulty we have with turning the other cheek (Matt. 5:39) . . . we don't know the half of it. The half-millionth of it.

But something about this singular event, this extremely not-nice way of handling a situation that struck Him wrong, seems to surprisingly remove anger from *our* no-no list too. And turn it into possibly a Christlike approach, say, addressing the teenage boys' garage band racket at the house next door.

Yet before we go all vigilante on people, we should probably stop seeing ourselves as the cheerleaders at Jesus' epic, biblical showdown, and consider instead whether our actual seat is with the mass merchants on the temple trading floor . . . guilty of some of the same things they were doing.

Here's what the historians tell us. People arriving in Jerusalem from out of town during this period of annual festival didn't commonly drag along their prescribed animal from home for sacrifice. They were counting on being able to buy one when they got there. But temple rules forbade the presence of anything pagan on its premises, including the type of images that appeared on the faces of Roman currency. So as a second part of this Passover transaction—before people could even purchase a suitable specimen to offer on the altar—they were forced to exchange their defiled coinage for another type of money that was free of any inscriptions promoting idolatry.

The whole thing was just ripe for swindling and profiteering. And apparently this money exchange/livestock auction had become such a booming business opportunity that its footprint had swelled to include the inner courts of the temple, right there inside the complex itself.

Church had become a good place to make a living. And making a good living had begun to take precedence over what this church place—and the God who owned it—was all about. As Jesus said (quoting Isaiah) in the midst of His stormy tirade, "It is written, 'My house will be called a house of prayer'" (Matt. 21:13).

But what place have *we* given in our hearts to such things as prayer and worship and godly devotion? And does it even hold a candle anymore to the place we've given in our hearts to money? To buying? To selling?

Or dare we call it . . . greed?

Anger with Sorrow

That's probably enough of a diagnostic question for now. We can just let it sit there, ready to be taken into our quiet moments with God where we go for in-depth reflection and soul-searching. If taken seriously enough, we might even pose it to the people who know us best, asking them to tell us—honestly now—if they see more love for Christ in our hearts than love for anything else.

God bless you for wanting to be pure in this matter.

But in those places where, yes, we recognize the envious clutches of greed in our lives, let's see if we can do more than just receive it as a divine rebuke. Let's see if we can learn something from Jesus' anger that can take us from merely being chastened to actually being changed.

Only in a few biblical spots is Jesus described as being angry. One occurred when the Pharisees challenged Him for daring to heal a man's paralyzed hand on the Sabbath. When they couldn't answer the following question—"Is it lawful on the Sabbath to do what is good or to do what is evil, to save life or to kill?" (Mark 3:4)—the Scripture says He glared at them with "anger and sorrow at the hardness of their hearts" (v. 5).

Anger. And sorrow. Together. Hmm.

But outside of the temple-cleansing episode (Matt. 21; Mark 11; Luke 19; John 2), the maddest we see Him anywhere else in the Bible was at the tomb of his friend Lazarus, brother of Mary and Martha. John's narrative of the event depicts the thick grief that pervaded the scene, even four days after Lazarus' death. Mary was crying. The other Jews who had come to visit were crying. But when John tried describing what he saw in *Jesus'* crying, he felt the need to use different, more passionate words altogether. "Jesus wept," of course (John 11:35)—that favorite two-word memory verse of smart-alecks everywhere—but His tears weren't just tears of sadness. "He was angry in His spirit and deeply moved" (v. 33). A little later,

John said He was "angry in Himself again" (v. 38), still not shaking the sense of anguish He was experiencing.

Anger. And sorrow. Coming together again.

Perhaps we can say, then, that Jesus' anger—even at the moneychangers in the temple—wasn't simply at the people themselves. It came from somewhere much deeper than that, a place where holy anger and godly sorrow can intermingle. For though He was looking at these people, He was also looking through them and over their heads, targeting a distant problem point that existed beyond the mere time-and-space location where this greedy, money-grubbing activity was right then occurring.

Jesus' anger at the tomb of Lazarus represented His indignation at what sin had brought into the world. At the reign of death that could wound people's hearts so painfully. And at the cost He already knew would be required of Him to pay, by means of a torturous execution, to reverse the agony that Satan's designs had inflicted on God's people and creation.

Could it be, then, that when you feel the sting of spiritual conviction over something like greed and envy or a minimizing of your love and thirst for Christ, His anger is not so much with *you*? (Bad you.) It's with the conniving, convincing voice of temptation that has tricked you into believing a lie: that you need money and more stuff, more than you need Him.

So while any twinge of guilt should send up warning flags in our hearts, leading us to want to purge the offense and walk again in purity, perhaps it's only in our selfishness that we take His correction so personally. Perhaps our anger too—like His—should be turned not into an open palm smacked hard against our forehead, but into a holy disdain for our spiritual enemy and for his ability to deceive us into accepting so much less for our lives than our God desires for us as His children.

When Jesus encountered the man most famously known to us as the rich young ruler—a man whose greed for his possessions prevented him from surrendering himself to Christ's lordship—the Bible says, "Looking at him, Jesus loved him" (Mark 10:21). *Loved him*—this man who, the last we saw of him, was slinking away in pride and disobedience. There's not much to love about him from our vantage point. But Jesus, in challenging the man's greed, didn't blast away at him with well-deserved anger. "Looking at him, Jesus loved him." Greed and all. Just as He loves you . . . and desires for you a better way forward than what money alone can ever provide.

Change for the Better

Getting real about the greed in our hearts is an incredible restarting place. A lot of us, like one of the two sons featured in a well-known parable of Jesus, have been slow to admit our problem and resistant to His correction. This young man's father had approached him one morning, saying, "Go, work in the vineyard today," to which he answered, "I don't want to!" But later he changed his mind, changed his clothes, and did what his dad had told him (Matt. 21:28–29). Then the father went to his other son and told him the same thing—to go work in the vineyard for the day. Although the second son piped up, "I will, sir" (v. 30), he didn't end up actually going, so . . .

"Which of the two," Jesus asked, "did his father's will?"

"The first," they said (v. 31)—the one who saw he'd been wrong, then did the right thing, the one who let conscience pull him out of a rut and back up on the road.

And that person can be us too . . . if we'll not become hopelessly, blindly, pridefully stuck in the sinful places where we've been living, and we'll begin courageously walking out of them toward the calling voice of Christ and His Word.

Asaph, the writer of Psalm 81, spoke of God, saying, "My people did not listen to Me; Israel did not obey Me. So I gave them over to their stubborn hearts to follow their own plans." But if only they *would* listen to Him, said the Lord, and "follow My ways, I would quickly subdue their enemies and turn My hand against their foes" (vv. 11–14).

"Quickly." Immediately.

Jesus doesn't really demand a giant leap of faith and repentance before He can *quickly* start showing you the difference between obedience and defiance, or even just plain indifference. "Whoever is faithful in very little"—in *very little*, He said—"is also faithful in much," just as "whoever is unrighteous in very little is also unrighteous in much" (Luke 16:10).

To further drive home His point, He turned to money as an example: "If you have not been faithful with the unrighteous money, who will trust you with what is genuine? And if you have not been faithful with what belongs to someone else, who will give you what is your own?" (vv. 11–12). But if, by contrast, we change our handling and attitude toward money—even by taking small, steady, deliberate steps in a positive direction—we will begin to see measurable growth and blessing as God produces the fruit of His righteous principles in our lives. Much quicker than we thought.

It's good-bye, greed; hello, gratitude.

And the great joy of bringing a smile to Jesus' face.

We don't know what became of the men whose portable offices in the temple were so violently shut down by Jesus' surprise inspection. We don't know all the heated meetings that took place in the aftermath, although we know within a week He'd been sentenced to death in a hasty trial and hauled outside the city amid a mob scene to the site of His bloody crucifixion.

But if any of those men had taken Jesus' angry warning to heart and seen the error of their greedy ways, they could've experienced—like you can experience—the joy of a changed life and the peaceful confidence that comes from overcoming sin and temptation.

"For God did not send His Son into the world that He might condemn the world," Jesus said, "but that the world might be saved through Him" (John 3:17).

Saved from everything that makes you so mad at yourself, by the One who's even angrier than you at what sin has done to hurt you.

For Family and Bible Study Discussion

1. What makes you angry? And what does your answer tell you about what you're truly passionate about?
2. How much guilt or shame do you feel over your financial attitudes or your history with money?
3. When or with whom does greed pose the greatest temptation to you?
4. What's a small start you could take toward overcoming what greed leads you to do?

Words of Jesus from this chapter—Matt. 21:13; Matt. 21:28–31; Luke 16:10–12; John 2:16; John 3:17

8

On Generosity

Cultivate a Give-First Mentality

*You have received free of charge; give
free of charge. (Matthew 10:8)*

Jesus was a master at telling stories and making analogies, of taking common, ordinary, household items and infusing them with spiritual meaning. One of the most versatile of these is a word picture He crafted about the difference between old and new *wineskins*.

Wine in Jesus' day was developed by letting it age and ferment within leather bags or pouches. But the various gases and chemical reactions that occurred during the process would cause expansion within the skins. After repeated use, these hearty containers would eventually lose the bulk of their elasticity, becoming brittle and starting to crack, to rupture. So if put into service one time too many, here's what Jesus said would happen: "The skins burst, the wine spills out, and the skins are ruined" (Matt. 9:17). Everything's a mess. A total loss.

That's why "new wine should be put into fresh wineskins" (Luke 5:38). Old wineskins, just like old ways of thinking, just like old ways of living—yes, even like old ways of handling and managing our money—simply aren't capable of housing "new wine." Once Christ and His Word and His Spirit are inside us, we're in for trouble if the wineskin of our lives doesn't change to match.

Now, speaking of old financial habits: among our most natural, instinctual, playground-level thoughts about money is that whatever we get is ours to keep. *Mine.* Not yours, not theirs, not anybody else's. We made it; we worked for it; we should be able to do whatever we want with it. Besides, who knows how much is ever enough? Don't want to get caught at the end of our lives without sufficient money to cover our expenses. Best thing we can do is to hang on to every penny we possibly can. Let everybody else worry about themselves.

Okay, so there you have it. That's an old wineskin talking. A combination of greed, distrust, worry, discontentment, with probably some touches of bitterness and anger thrown in—none of the things that come together to form what any of us would call Christlike thinking and behavior. And while people who operate in this fashion may amass a great deal of interest-bearing securities and all, there's a Scrooge-like payoff in the end that cannot help but result in a weathered, cracked wineskin of a life. Sour to the taste.

But as believers, we are recipients of something new and different—the presence of Christ—being continually informed by His teachings and fueled by His abundant life. This means we must let Him make us new and different ourselves. Otherwise, we'll be repeatedly leaking from the seams, from the soles, and from everywhere else—if we don't strip off this old, stingy, grabby way of living and give Him a new, fresh wineskin to inhabit, one that can freely receive and respond to such instructions from Him as . . .

"Give to one who asks you, and don't turn away from the one who wants to borrow from you" (Matt. 5:42).

"Sell your possessions and give to the poor" (Luke 12:33).

"Whoever gives just a cup of cold water to one of these little ones because he is a disciple—I assure you: He will never lose his reward!" (Matt. 10:42).

"You have received free of charge; give free of charge" (Matt. 10:8), for as Paul reported Jesus as saying, "It is more blessed to give than to receive'" (Acts 20:35).

See the difference? There's just no putting that kind of Christ-centered, God-honoring freedom and generosity into a heart that won't flex and adapt to it. We'll be fighting it all the time. Prickling up against whatever He's telling us to do, not wanting to do it. And that is not a winning combination in a Christian's life.

But just imagine . . . imagine inhaling and exhaling in deep, contented agreement with Him, accepting that what Jesus said about our hearts and our money is the purest, sweetest, most joyous way to live. That's how we'd experience the fullness of what He came to do in us. That's how the flavor and aroma of Christ would begin to emanate from our lives, from our faces, from our families, from our churches . . . when everything about us is reflecting the give-first mentality He's taught us and showed us how to live.

A Giving Heart

From the outside looking in, people might think *giving* is the only use for money that Jesus approves. Hopefully we've seen and read enough by now to realize this isn't true. But giving is certainly foundational to the heart of God and should therefore be a square-one component of ours as well. To quote perhaps the most well-known example: "God loved the world in this way: He gave His One and Only Son, so that everyone who believes in Him will . . . have eternal life" (John 3:16).

Giving is central to the gospel.

Giving is at the core of Christian living.

But maybe the reason why giving our *money* can be sometimes so downright painful to us—turning loose of that twenty that could've been, what, maybe three or four lunches this week?—is because giving money isn't where giving begins. It's where it leads. Giving starts from a giving heart. Then money becomes just one of giving's many expressions.

Jesus taught us, for instance, to have a giving heart for the *hurting*. Several verses into Matthew 14, we find Him getting word about the savage beheading of John the Baptist, the one who bravely foretold Jesus' physical arrival as the Lamb of God. Jesus was obviously moved by this happening, deciding to withdraw by boat to a remote place, wanting to be alone to pray. But no sooner had He stepped ashore than the crowds scampered to get close to Him, and He responded as He, of course, would: "He saw a huge crowd, felt compassion for them, and healed their sick" (v. 14)—a picture of His giving heart.

After a long day, however, darkness began approaching, and the disciples sought to head off an approaching problem. They came up to Jesus and said, "This place is a wilderness, and it is already late. Send the crowds away so they can go into the villages and buy food for themselves" (v. 15)—a picture of *their* heart. As far as the disciples were concerned, these people needed to move on, all right? *Their problems are not our problem*, they seemed to be saying.

But, no, "they don't need to go away," Jesus said to them. "You give them something to eat" (v. 16).

You can almost see the stares of stunned disbelief among His tight group of followers. You can hear the pause of look-around silence, perhaps the breath of an escaped laugh from one of them, like, "Is He kidding?" *Us? Huh? Do what now?*

Okay, let's give them a bit of a break here. Five thousand people, probably many more. "Should we go and buy 200 denarii worth of bread and give them something to eat?" they asked, rather sarcastically (Mark 6:37). But understandably. The impossibility of what Jesus was suggesting easily invited this kind of skepticism. But while His disciples apparently weren't at the point yet of realizing that Jesus could turn a young boy's lunch into twelve baskets of leftovers, one thing He was trying to establish within them was this: a heart that looks first to see how you can *help* before conveniently deciding to pass. For when Jesus is in the picture, you simply don't know what will happen once the giving starts. You only know what will happen if you don't.

He also taught us to have a giving heart of *forgiveness*. He told a parable about a king whose servant owed him an enormous debt, more than he could possibly repay in a lifetime.

Yet the servant begged for mercy, asked for more time. And the king, against all logic, "had compassion, released him, and forgave him the loan" (Matt. 18:27). Bad news, though, when such incredible wine strikes the inside of an old wineskin. This very servant, who was owed a much, much smaller sum by one of his fellow slaves, went out and demanded immediate repayment. "He grabbed him, started choking him, and said, 'Pay what you owe!'" (v. 28).

This insight into the heart of God, the heart of man, and what Jesus expects of His people gave a dramatic answer to Peter's earlier question: "Lord, how many times could my brother sin against me and I forgive him? As many as seven times?" No, Jesus said, "not as many as seven . . . but 70 times seven" (vv. 21–22). Here's the takeaway: be looking to find points of restoration and healing rather than simply finding fault. *Do what a giving heart does.*

Because when a giving heart meets human need, human hurting, human sorrow, human despair, it follows Christ into the situation . . . and starts pouring out new wine in whatever form He leads us to take.

Pure Giving

Jesus' parable of the Good Samaritan is a classic example of this expectation—and a revealing, convicting critique of what happens when those who claim to be God's people look like old wineskins in sheep's clothing.

Let's look at the ugly part of the story first, because Jesus had already spent a good portion of His time reprimanding the religious elites and establishment for being all talk and no compassion. He once called them out, for instance, by telling them, "You say, 'Whoever tells his father or mother, "Whatever benefit you might have received from me is a gift committed to the temple"—he does not have to honor his father.' In this way, you have revoked God's word because of your tradition" (Matt. 15:5–6). "You pay a tenth of mint, dill, and cumin, yet you have neglected the more important matters of the law—justice, mercy, and faith. These things should have been done without neglecting the others" (23:23).

There's your backdrop, then, for Jesus' fictional portrayals of the priest and the Levite—two religious professionals who happened upon the man knocked half dead by robbers and just piously, heartlessly, "passed by on the other side" (Luke 10:32). No muss, no fuss. Things to do, places to go, people to see and be seen by.

"But a Samaritan on his journey came up to him, and when he saw the man, he had compassion" (v. 33)—a word we've heard Jesus speak more than once in this chapter. "He went over to him and bandaged his wounds, pouring on olive oil and wine. Then he put him on his own animal, brought him to an inn, and took care of him" (v. 34). What a guy, this caring Samaritan.

So it's only natural—well within the flow of his compassion—when we see him in the next verse reaching into his wallet, handing a few dollars to the innkeeper, and saying, "Take care of him. When I come back I'll reimburse you for whatever extra you spend" (v. 35). The Samaritan wasn't just a good man who somewhere along the line had made a commitment to being more generous with his money. He'd cultivated a heart of giving and charity. He was a give-first person. And by being one of these, it sincerely changed how he chose to view and handle his money—simply as yet another means of showing true compassion.

Jesus said when we do this, we're not just helping people. We're not just giving a handout or buying a meal or putting toys under a little kid's Christmas tree. "When the Son of Man comes in His glory, and all the angels with Him . . . all the nations will be gathered before Him, and He will separate them one from another" (Matt. 25:31–32). Then He will invite those who are truly His followers to "inherit the kingdom prepared for you from the foundation of the world. For I was hungry and you gave Me something to eat; I was thirsty and you gave Me something to drink; I was a stranger and you took Me in; I was naked and you clothed Me; I was sick and you took care of Me; I was in prison and you visited Me" (vv. 34–36).

"Then the righteous will answer Him, 'Lord, when did we see You hungry . . . thirsty . . . a stranger . . . without clothes . . . sick, or in prison, and visit You?' And the King will answer them, 'I assure you: Whatever you did to the least of these brothers of Mine, you did for Me'" (vv. 37–40).

They did it for Him.

You're doing it . . . for Him.

The One who gave "His life—a ransom for many" (Mark 10:45).

A ransom for you. So that you can now give. To others. To Him.

For Family and Bible Study Discussion

1. How difficult or natural does giving come to you?
2. Think of a Good Samaritan situation you recently faced. How did you handle it? What ran through your mind at the time?
3. Realizing that every gift is spiritually a gift to Jesus, how does this truth influence your desire to be more freely generous?
4. What are some regular, deliberate, ongoing giving opportunities that could come together into a giving plan for you?

Words of Jesus from this chapter—Matt. 5:42; Matt. 9:17; Matt. 10:8; Matt. 10:42; Matt. 14:14–16; Matt. 15:5–6; Matt. 18:21–22; Matt 18:27–28; Matt. 23:23; Matt. 25:31–40; Mark 6:37; Mark 10:45; Luke 5:38; Luke 10:32–35; Luke 12:33; John 3:16; Acts 20:35

9

On Sacrifice

Give to People Who Can't Pay You Back

*For you will be repaid at the resurrection
of the righteous. (Luke 14:14)*

A s a rule, we don't live on the edge enough.

But if we ever did, we'd never want to come back. Far too much of our Christian life is spent in the safe zone of cautious decisions, practical efficiency, measured responses, and overprotectiveness. Not that any of those things are ridiculous ways of handling certain situations. But when they add up to the sum total of our everyday business, we sure do limit some openings that could keep us in perpetual awe of God and of His power at work in us.

For example, most people's level of giving to the church is the five- or ten- or twenty-dollar variety. Whatever bill's in our wallet when they pass the plate around. Whichever one leaves us enough cash to buy lunch on the way home. But the average giving of the average churchgoer is typically a low, low percentage of his or her weekly income. Somewhere in the 1 to 2 to 3 percent range.

Now, for everyone's information, the biblical standard throughout the Old Testament was the tithe, or tenth (featured most notably in Malachi 3:10—"Bring the full tenth into the storehouse"). Jesus, too, though He never came out and declared what our giving expectation should be, implied His endorsement of the tithing practice in His challenge to the Pharisees in Luke 11:42. ("These things you should have done"—the payment of the "tenth"—without ignoring "justice and love for God.")

Yet whenever He commented on how we should apply the Old Testament law to our New Testament lives, the general takeaway of His teaching was to say we should *surpass* it. "You have heard that it was said to our ancestors, 'Do not murder,' and whoever murders will be subject to judgment. But I tell you, everyone who is angry with his brother will be subject to judgment" (Matt. 5:21–22). Raising the benchmark.

Do not commit adultery? "I tell you, everyone who looks at a woman to lust for her has already committed adultery in his heart" (v. 28). *An eye for an eye, a tooth for a tooth?* "On the contrary, if anyone slaps you on your right cheek, turn the other to him also" (v. 39). *Love your neighbor?* Yes, of course, but also "love your enemies" (v. 44).

Go beyond. Do more. "For I tell you, unless your righteousness surpasses that of the scribes and Pharisees, you will never enter the kingdom of heaven" (v. 20).

Now if you're not accustomed to giving a tithe, doing so would likely create a shock to the system. Though biblical and obedient, it would still be a bold increase. Raising your giving level to 10 percent would be a noticeable sacrifice to your current budget and lifestyle spending decisions. It might take you to the edge—where (to quote from Malachi 3:10 again), God says, "Test Me in this way. . . . See if I will not open the floodgates of heaven and pour out a blessing for you without measure."

But what if you're already giving the tithe, an offering that the Old Testament often describes with the word *firstfruits*—coming right off the top, before anything else? What if you responded to God's Spirit by committing to give 12 percent? Or 15 percent? Or more? Until it represented for you a real sacrifice, same as going from 5 up to 10 percent might feel for someone else? What might happen out on the edge of your faith *then*? What kind of adventure of spiritual growth and opportunity might God choose to take you and your family on, building on your increased level of invested faith and money into His kingdom mission?

Amazing to think about.

But it takes a sacrifice to get there. Sacrifice is built in to abundant Christian living. Not because God enjoys turning the screws on us, but because He knows—in His strong, loving, all-knowing, all-everything hands—any sacrifice of ours is actually an anti-sacrifice. For as Jesus said, "Give, and it will be given to you: a good measure—pressed down, shaken together, and running over—will be poured into your lap. For with the measure you use, it will be measured back to you" (Luke 6:38).

But only those who do it will find out.

The rest are too scared to try.

Adventures in Giving

Many of Jesus' teachings, as we've seen, were told in the form of parables. But He also taught by just pointing to the real-world events that were happening around Him and telling people to take closer notice, to see what God could communicate through the lens of others' lives.

During the final few days before His trial, beating, and death—when sacrifice was very much on His mind—Jesus was sitting with His disciples in the temple courts, most likely what was known as the Court of the Women, so named because that was as close as women could come to the sanctuary. The temple treasury was located there. It consisted of thirteen chests or receptacles that each contained a fluted, metallic opening—shaped sort of like a trumpet—where coins deposited into it would clang around and echo across the courtyard, like the ring of a cash register. Perfect for making a dramatic, resounding show of one's, uh . . . holiness.

So in this very teachable moment, Jesus was watching "how the crowd dropped money into the treasury. Many rich people were putting in large sums" (Mark 12:41). But His eye was drawn to a poor widow who "came and dropped in two tiny coins worth very little" (v. 42). No cha-ching. No ring-up. Just the nearly inaudible tink-tink of her thin little coins, lost among all the heavy currency at the bottom of the bucket.

But her gift wasn't lost on Jesus. Motioning to His disciples, He said to them, "I assure you: This poor widow has put in more than all those giving to the temple treasury. For they all gave out of their surplus, but she out of her poverty has put in everything she possessed—all she had to live on" (vv. 43–44).

Or as the old saying goes, the chicken may make a *contribution* to a bacon-and-eggs breakfast, but the pig makes a *sacrifice*.

A second current event of equal surprise and importance had occurred not long beforehand in the Jordan Valley town of Jericho, one of the oldest cities in the world. Jesus was passing through the area. He was a very well-known figure by that time. And among those who were trying to get a closer look at Him was a "wee little man" named Zacchaeus, the wizened tax collector who famously shinnied up a sycamore tree so he could peer over the tops of his neighbors' heads. We all know most of the story from there—how Jesus looked up, saw him, and said to him, "Zacchaeus, hurry and come down because today I must stay at your house" (Luke 19:5).

Lots of lessons here, obviously, such as how Jesus treated what the world called "sinful" men (v. 7), as opposed to, I guess, people who *aren't* sinful? Or so they thought. But the most notable application from this story is a lesson in sacrifice—how a rich businessman whose heart was transformed through a personal encounter with Jesus was moved to "give half of my possessions to the poor, Lord! And if I have extorted anything from anyone"—*yeah, if?*—"I'll pay back four times as much!" (v. 8).

What a change. What a difference. A rich man going beyond normal worship, gratitude, and generosity, just like the poor widow at the temple. "Today salvation has come to this house," Jesus said of Zacchaeus, "for the Son of Man has come to seek and to save the lost" (vv. 9–10)—to show us by *His* sacrifice the incredible things He can do through *our* sacrifice.

To the Edge

No weirder than someone's idea that they can be "good enough" to earn God's heavenly favor is the Christian's idea that his or her perfunctory, painless level of sacrifice ought to be "good enough" to get the job done, now that he or she is already in the club. *No.* "If anyone wants to be My follower," Jesus said, "he must deny himself, take up his cross, and follow Me" (Mark 8:34). Not simply at first, but for the long haul. Let's not just skip over these lines as though they're amped-up, overzealous exaggerations . . . or worse, because we consider our current level of self-denial probably all He really meant by that.

Probably not. We will always tend to hold back when it hurts, to encircle ourselves with whatever makes us comfortable. But when Jesus told a tentative, hesitant follower how "foxes have dens and birds have nests, but the Son of Man has no place to lay His head" (Matt. 8:20), He wasn't talking in generalities. He was stating a fact. He was laying down the expectation of radical change and difference. As He said to His disciples at their last meal together, after He'd broken with all form and tradition by stooping down before them with basin and towel, "If I, your Lord and Teacher, have washed your feet, you also ought to wash one another's feet. For I have given you an example that you also should do just as I have done for you" (John 13:14–15).

We are meant to serve. Like Jesus served. We are meant to give. Like Jesus gave. When He said to the Pharisees (who considered Him a lawbreaker for not following the rules), "I desire mercy and not sacrifice" (Matt. 9:13), He meant that denying yourself to serve others is actually a lot more of a sacrifice than merely checking off some religious do-good box and feeling so righteous for it.

He's calling us to the edge.

Out where we don't reserve our kindness only for people who are kind back to us. "For if you love those who love you, what reward will you have? Don't even the tax collectors do the same?" (Matt. 5:46).

Out where we don't just hang around exclusively with people who think and act like we do. "If you greet only your brothers, what are you doing out of the ordinary? Don't even the Gentiles do the same?" (v. 47).

Out where we don't guard our money so tightly that we only give to those who are assured of paying us back. "If you lend to those from whom you expect to receive, what credit is that to you? Even sinners lend to sinners to be repaid in full" (Luke 6:34).

Out where we don't give merely in exchange for other people's approval and admiration of our godly reputation. "Be careful not to practice your righteousness in front of people, to be seen by them. Otherwise, you will have no reward from your Father in heaven. So whenever you give to the poor," Jesus continued, "don't sound a trumpet before you, as the hypocrites do in the synagogues and on the streets, to be applauded by people. I assure you: They've got their reward! But when you give to the poor, don't let your left hand know what your right hand is doing, so that your giving may be in secret. And your Father who sees in secret will reward you" (Matt. 6:1–4).

Once when Jesus was visiting in the home of one of the leading Pharisees, He noticed the attention-getting self-importance of those who'd been invited, how they hobnobbed with the people they most wanted to impress, enjoying the customary scratch-my-back-I'll-scratch-yours kind of mutual admiration society. Jesus wanted to shake this up a little, so He took the occasion to say to the one who'd asked Him to come, "When you give a lunch or a dinner, don't invite your friends, your brothers, your relatives, or your rich neighbors, because they might invite you back, and you would be repaid. On the contrary, when you host a banquet, invite those who are poor, maimed, lame, or blind. And you will be blessed, because they cannot repay you; for you will be repaid at the resurrection of the righteous" (Luke 14:12–14).

Think Jesus knows what He's talking about? Knows what it's like to give people something they can't possibly repay? And knows the unparalleled joy of seeing His sacrifice result in life-changing blessing and goodness for those to whom He's given Himself so freely?

He must want us to know some of that same feeling and experience too. And so He invites us to the edge. To what some people would consider needless, foolish sacrifice. But only because they don't know what it's like to be paid back in heavenly currency.

For Family and Bible Study Discussion

1. How sacrificial would you say your level of giving is?
2. What have you observed about the lives of those who give in sacrificial ways?
3. Why is giving to your church a foundational component of your overall giving?
4. What might a deeper commitment to giving do to counteract any sense of dullness, boredom, or irrelevance you sense about your spiritual life?

Words of Jesus from this chapter—Matt. 5:20–22; Matt. 5:28; Matt. 5:39; Matt. 5:44; Matt. 5:46–47; Matt. 6:1–4; Matt. 8:20; Matt. 9:13; Mark 8:34; Mark 12:41–44; Luke 6:34; Luke 6:38; Luke 14:12–14; Luke 19:9–10; John 13:14–15

10

On Comparisons

Money Is Not a Measuring Stick

*Are you jealous because I'm
generous? (Matthew 20:15)*

W ho is rich?" That was the question asked in
a *Washington Post* survey to a wide swath of
respondents, covering pretty much the full range
of economic strata. And their answers generally scaled up or
down depending on their own level of income. People living
in households earning less than $50,000 a year, for example,
said they would consider someone rich if they were making a
couple hundred thousand. Those whose earnings placed them
in the next higher-up income bracket raised the threshold of
annual wealth to an average of around $260k. And for those
families already pulling down combined salaries in excess of
$100,000, the definition of rich meant making a cool half-
million. Or, of course, more.

Basically, then, the people we think of as rich are people
who make more than *we* do. That's sort of the bottom-line

sentiment. That's what we're shooting for. Or at least wishing for. Across the board. And presumably across the world.

Because if $200,000 or $500,000 sounds "rich" in a country like the United States, where the median yearly household income is just north of $40,000, what about in a place like Sierra Leone ($2,300 per annum in US equivalent) or Zambia ($1,500) or Liberia (just $780)? Most likely a family in one of those countries would be deemed seriously rich if they were making, what—$15,000 or so? Though in America this same level of income would place them under the federal poverty level. It's all kind of relative like that.

So our definition of wealth is not really a specific number. It's a number in relation to *our* number. A race against our friends and fellow man. A competition between winners and losers. A test that determines who's making it and who's not.

And to Jesus, this whole comparison contest is a total waste of time.

Because, yes, He admitted to His disciples, the world around them was (and would always be) dog-eat-dog, a daily battle, where brother challenges brother, where people are constantly trying to beat others to the top, even if it occasionally requires pushing others down to get there. Yet He instructed them (and us) not to fear these other people— their power over us, their competitive leg up on us, their smug satisfaction in outperforming us, or whatever they do to try to intimidate us and come out ahead of us—but rather to fear only God, to whom everyone on the earth must answer and to whom none of us, not the last single one of us, is superior.

For like John the Baptist had said, quoting from the prophet Isaiah, the coming of Jesus leveled the playing field between ourselves and others. "Every valley will be filled"—no one beneath all hope of being redeemed through the gospel—"every mountain and hill will be made low"—no one having earned the right to His favor through their pedigree or performance (Luke 3:5).

And that makes all the other little competitions and comparisons that go on between us—they all amount to the proverbial deck-chair arrangements on the *Titanic*. Seemingly important in the moment, as far as who gets to be seen sitting by whom, but ultimately as trivial and irrelevant as anything could possibly be.

So as a grace-based, faith-filled follower of Jesus, you can just rest now, knowing you have already been infused through Christ with incredible worth and value. "Aren't two sparrows sold for a penny?" He said. "Yet not one of them falls to the ground without your Father's consent. But even the hairs of your head have all been counted. So don't be afraid therefore; you are worth more than many sparrows" (Matt. 10:29–31). Worth so much more than you realize. Without needing to be sized up (or sized down) alongside anyone else.

Eliminating the Competition

This inclination toward making comparisons with others comes rather standard on the human model. It doesn't take us long on the birthday-party circuit before we realize there's a difference between the kinds of toys all the other kids get and the ones that idly hang out in our own boring closet back home.

And what starts between ages three and five becomes an art form by the time we reach adulthood. We develop an almost involuntary reflex of noticing the cuff links, the pressed creases, the manicure, the car in the driveway. The sags of skin at the neck or the lines around the eyes. *(Wonder how old she is?)* The comparative size of someone else's lot space and square footage, their kitchen appliances and television set. Even our own children become currency in this contest of achievement, scored by talent and activity schedules, by titles and personal rankings, then later by the kinds of careers they undertake and the level of advancement they obtain. Enter the annual family Christmas letter into the record as Exhibit A.

But comparisons are pointless. And according to Jesus, impermissible. "Do not judge, so that you won't be judged. For with the judgment you use, you will be judged, and with the measure you use, it will be measured to you" (Matt. 7:1–2). And since we've been given this prohibition—this warning against judging ourselves in competition with others—there must be a way out of it. Out of this comparison cycle.

Yes, there is. And it starts by changing how we determine what's truly valuable—first, by truly seeing ourselves as sinners, no better off than anyone else in God's eyes; yet second, realizing the ultimate value of our rescue in Christ, which leaves us with nothing more to be attained. Because now that we've been welcomed into personal relationship with the One who owns "every animal of the forest" and the "cattle on a thousand hills," our only proper response toward whatever relative circumstances we're experiencing in life should be bringing a "thank offering" to Him (Ps. 50:10, 14)—being continually grateful to Him—not quibbling among ourselves to see whose house, job, jewelry, wardrobe, technology gadgets, or (insert additional items here) is more showy, impressive, desirable, exotic, artistic, expensive, or (insert additional adjectives here).

The trappings just really don't mean that much, you know? Nor do they tell the whole story anyway.

The prodigal son in Jesus' parable had money. Lots of money. Rich enough to wow a whole bunch of people who probably thought, boy, wish they had his kind of bankroll. But before long, after he had "spent everything" and after "a severe famine struck," Jesus said the young man was left with "nothing" (Luke 15:14)—which was really all he had from the very beginning, even when he seemed to have everything. The only wealth he experienced was actually found in his poverty—in buckling under the weight of his own sin, seeing himself for who he really was, then returning to his father in humility and repentance. Money was *completely* the wrong measuring stick for ascertaining his success or failure as an individual, right?

As it is with everyone.

"A tree is known by its fruit," Jesus said (Matt. 12:33). *That's it.* The only thing we ought to be recognizing and hoping to emulate in others is the good fruit that grows from their good heart. "A good man produces good things from his storeroom of good," Jesus said, "and an evil man produces evil things from his storeroom of evil" (v. 35).

So there's nothing wrong with inspecting others' fruit production, or with inviting people to carefully inspect and evaluate ours. In fact, doing so is probably a fairly healthy practice. The "do not judge" command of Jesus doesn't mean we're not supposed to look, to notice anybody, or to form opinions that might prove helpful or instructive, both to ourselves and others. Nor does it absolve us from the responsibility for taking regular, routine stock of our own motives, behaviors, blind spots, and sincerity levels. But even then, our purpose behind being observant and cognizant of what's going on around us should not be to *compare* ourselves with anybody—on any subject matter or standard of judgment—but rather to be helping each other live out the gospel, to put forth a compellingly genuine witness for Christ, and to bring glory to God as He transforms our lives into something beautifully and bountifully fruit-bearing.

Comparing is just a bad business.

Fair Enough

Perhaps the most direct teaching of Jesus on this subject of comparisons came through His parable of the vineyard workers. A landowner, He said, "went out early in the morning to hire workers for his vineyard" (Matt. 20:1). Each agreed to work for one denarius—the common wage for a full day's manual labor. But a little later in the morning, the businessman noticed some people still standing around in the marketplace, having so far been unable to find work for the day. He said to them, "You also go to my vineyard, and I'll give you whatever is right" (v. 4).

Again at noon, then again at three, the landowner rounded up fresh workers from the available pool of candidates. Even as late as five, not long before quitting time, he gathered up more men and sent them out to finish up the day. At least they could put in an hour or so.

So in wave after wave, these new shifts had been arriving at his property. All day long. Some had worked from morning till night, while others had barely been there long enough to work up a sweat. But at the close of business that evening, when the foreman called everyone in to receive their payment, he gave each person a denarius, regardless of the hours they'd invested.

Whoa, whoa, *whoa!* cried the guys who'd been there since sunrise. "These last men put in one hour, and you made them equal to us who bore the burden of the day and the burning heat!" (v. 12). But wasn't the landowner only giving these original hires what they'd agreed to work for? Hadn't they been happy at six that morning just to land a job? And comfortable at the time with what he was offering? The only difference between the denarius they'd *expected* and the denarius they actually *received* was in how it compared now to everybody else's. But when we're focused on the wrong thing—on money instead of on the giver, on money instead of on our faithfulness to the task—this distance can often be the difference between gratitude and bitterness.

"Take what's yours and go," the owner of the vineyard told them. "I want to give this last man the same as I gave you. Don't I have the right to do what I want with my business? Are you jealous because I'm generous?" (vv. 14–15).

The answer to the first question? An absolute yes.

The answer to the second question? Had better be no.

Because the only thing we should really be "jealous" for is that God puts us to work in His vineyard, that He appropriates our lives for His purposes and generates glory for Himself from what we do and who we are. When Jesus' disciples asked Him about a blind man they passed on the side of the road—"Who sinned, this man or his parents, that he was born blind?"—He answered them, "Neither this man nor his parents sinned. This came about so that God's works might be displayed in him" (John 9:2–3). So whether we're crazy rich or barely getting by—or anywhere comparatively in between—no one is better off than when he or she is completely at peace with knowing that the Lord is in charge of everything. And of everybody. And is giving us everything we need for being useful and obedient to Him.

There is no comparison to that.

In one of Jesus' final conversations with His disciples, He took the opportunity to give Peter a heavy heads-up on what the future held for this impetuous, important apostle. "When you were young, you would tie your belt and walk wherever you wanted. But when you grow old, you will stretch out your hands and someone else will tie you and carry you where you don't want to go." Jesus said this, the Gospel writer added, "to signify by what kind of death [Peter] would glorify God," and to personally exhort him, eye to eye, to "Follow Me!" (John 21:18–19). *You can do this! I'll be there for you to see you through!*

Peter's first response, upon trying to absorb the prediction of this hard news, was to spin around and point a deflective, no-fair finger toward his buddy John, who was trailing along behind them at a bit of a distance, though apparently within earshot. "What about him?" Peter asked (v. 21). *It's not just me, is it? If I'm getting strung up for being Your follower, he's going down, too, isn't he?*

"If I want him to remain until I come," Jesus answered, "what is that to you? As for you"—Jesus' challenge remained the same—"follow Me" (v. 22).

Just keep following Me . . . regardless.

And don't worry about following what's happening with everyone else.

The comparisons simply don't do anybody any good.

For Family and Bible Study Discussion

1. Who is rich? And how did you arrive at your answer?
2. What are some of the most prominent ways you tend to compare yourself to others?
3. What would you describe as some of the most desirable "fruit" a Christian can grow?
4. What makes comparison such an endless game and pursuit?

Words of Jesus from this chapter—Matt. 7:1–2; Matt. 10:29–31; Matt. 12:33, 35; Matt. 20:1–15; Luke 15:14; John 9:3; John 21:18, 22

11

On Wisdom

Handle Your Money with Shrewd Integrity

*Give back to Caesar the things that are Caesar's,
and to God the things that are God's. (Mark 12:17)*

The Bible—the story of God's reaching out in love and power to redeem His fallen people—represents the fulfillment of a plan. A plan that originated in the mind and heart of God. A plan that will continue unfolding until "the kingdoms of this world are become the kingdoms of our Lord, and of his Christ; and he shall reign for ever and ever" (Rev. 11:15 KJV).

Our God is a planner, who also knows "the plans I have for you," He says, "plans for your welfare, not for disaster, to give you a future and a hope" (Jer. 29:11). And since He's created us in His image, we know He's also given us the strategy skills and inspiration to make plans for ourselves and to carry them out under His wise leadership, care, and provision.

So living without a financial plan is not faith.

It's more akin to foolishness.

"For which of you," Jesus asked, "wanting to build a tower, doesn't first sit down and calculate the cost to see if he has enough to complete it? Otherwise, after he has laid the foundation and cannot finish it, all the onlookers will begin to make fun of him. . . . Or what king, going to war against another king, will not first sit down and decide if he is able with 10,000 to oppose the one who comes against him with 20,000?" (Luke 14:28–29, 31).

Planning and looking ahead are Christ-centered things to do.

The Bible says Jesus spoke this particular teaching to large crowds who'd begun to travel with Him everywhere He went. And in making these statements, He mainly wanted them to realize that discipleship was a serious, sober, significant undertaking, not just a "hey, let's try that for a while, see if it works" kind of thing. No, it's a long-term, lifelong commitment. With weighty implications. Following Him is serious business, not just Sunday school class. We need to make sure we don't treat Him lightly or fail to recognize the high cost and comprehensive life cycle of being a devoted Christian.

But godly stewardship of our money is serious and long-term as well. It's a big deal. It matters. People's lives, whole generations—our children, our grandchildren—can either be blessed or depleted by how well or how weakly we do it. So we're not just playing around here. Saving, budgeting, giving, economizing—we need to be handling these ordinary household issues with thoughtful planning, with wise counsel, with careful contingencies, and with steady goals kept faithfully over time. With ample amounts of responsibility and lots of good teaching and training examples for the kids.

Not because money is the most important thing in the world, but because God has chosen for us to *live* in this world, and to represent Him well in everything we do.

Take, for example, the time when a handful of Jewish representatives accosted Peter, asking him whether Jesus had any intention of paying the "double-drachma tax" (Matt. 17:24). This wasn't actually a government tax, but rather a customary, religious collection taken from all Jewish males. The monies went toward supporting the temple and related expenses. Still, it was expected. Unofficially required and obligatory. Yet Jesus, when Peter came to Him reporting what the men had said, asked, "What do you think, Simon? Who do earthly kings collect tariffs or taxes from? From their sons or from strangers?"

"From strangers," Peter answered.

"Then the sons are free," Jesus said (vv. 25–26). Sounds like a no. As children of God, our only obligation is to Him, not to religious tradition.

"But," He said, "so we won't offend them" (v. 27), He instructed Peter to go pay enough double-drachma tax money for the both of them. (He did it by telling him to go locate the coin inside of a fish's belly, which is a cool story in itself, although probably best saved for another book so we can stay on topic here.)

The point being—no, Christians are not bound by the same things that confine everyone else: we don't need to please other people to be accepted; don't need to pay dues to be righteous; don't need to dance to anybody's tune just because everybody else is doing it. But to keep from fouling the waters that could pollute a relationship, or to avoid letting a small issue become a dug-in, overblown, unnecessary reason for people to tarnish believers' reputations, we are free to do things we're not *required* to do in order to maintain the respect of outsiders.

Like "Doc" Brown said in *Back to the Future*: "Roads? Where we're going, we don't *need* roads."

"Money? Where we're going, we don't *need* money."

But here, we honor God by being wise with money.

Better Business

Probably one of Jesus' most confusing, controversial parables fits well into our discussion at this point: the parable of the dishonest manager. A rich man had gotten wind of a report that one of his employees—the person he'd appointed to handle his business affairs—was cooking the books somehow. Funny business. So he called the man into his office and said, "What is this I hear about you? Give an account of your management, because you can no longer be my manager" (Luke 16:2).

Apparently the guy tap-danced well enough during the meeting to buy himself a second chance, but he knew he needed to act fast if he wanted to keep his job. "So he summoned each one of his master's debtors," and asked them, "How much do you owe my master?" (v. 5). If they said "a hundred measures of olive oil" (v. 6), he told them to mark it down to fifty. If they said "a hundred measures of wheat" (v. 7), he told them to knock it down to eighty.

Scholars who know how business was conducted during this period of history say the man was probably doing one of three or four things, either (a) actually dropping the price, (b) removing interest charges, (c) cancelling his commission on the transactions, or (d) reducing the debt down to what it should have been anyway before he'd overcharged them. Whichever one it was, when he delivered to his boss the cash that he'd quickly collected from these clients and customers, the only one who was losing money in the deal was the crooked manager himself. (As it should have been.)

So "the master praised the unrighteous manager because he had acted astutely" (v. 8)—even though there were plenty of things about the way this guy conducted his financial dealings that were *not* praiseworthy. And while Jesus—who began to apply some lessons from this story in the second half of verse 8—certainly wasn't condoning shady business practices, He did say "the sons of this age are more astute than the sons of light in dealing with their own people." In fact, He said to "make friends for yourselves by means of the unrighteous money so that when it fails, they may welcome you into eternal dwellings" (v. 9).

Make friends? With money? Huh?

Use it to get what you want from people?

Wasn't that basically what the prodigal son did?

We'll come back to this shocking statement in a second.

But this actually wasn't the first time He'd told His followers to look a little more street-smart. When He earlier had sent them out on their inaugural mission to announce "the kingdom of heaven has come near" (Matt. 10:7), He warned them, "Look, I'm sending you out like sheep among wolves.

Therefore be as shrewd as serpents and as harmless as doves"
(v. 16). It's not that He wanted them to trick or badger people
into believing the Messiah was now here among them. They
weren't supposed to stir up trouble. But neither should they
expect to be believed or received well everywhere they went.
And like a snake with the ability to slither out of danger and
keep itself from being caught, they needed to learn on the fly
how to implement some quick-thinking survival skills on the
road.

So back to Luke 16 now and the sleazy guy in the
accounting department. No, don't be him. But no, don't be
stupid. Use your money to help accomplish the objectives of a
believer. Make friends. Buy things from people. Buy things *for*
people. Sponsor a Little League team. Throw a block party.
Purchase your neighborhood children's Girl Scout cookies and
school fund-raising products. Don't just sit there, thinking
the only holy thing you can do with your money is to put
it in the collection plate at church. Use your imagination to
unlock doors that Christ can then enter to bring people into
His kingdom.

Sounds sneaky and manipulative to me. No, it's not
manipulation, unless you're doing it for all the wrong reasons.
It's simply making wise financial investments in the things
that are supposed to matter most to you.

Wise Differences

The theme that runs throughout this whole area of
thought is the age-old analysis of wisdom versus foolishness—a

discussion topic as old as the Proverbs and pervasive enough to run high and low throughout the Scriptures.

One of Jesus' parables, for instance, compared five wise and five foolish women participating in a typical marriage custom of the day. As friends of the wedding party, they went out to meet the groom, who was supposed to be coming from his home to the house of the bride, where the marriage would be celebrated. But the groom didn't come when they expected. The hour grew late. And with the party dying down, they all became tired and fell asleep.

Then—in the middle of the night—a shout arose that the groom was near, approaching. He was almost there. Five of the women trimmed their lamps and woke up to watch for him. But the other five hadn't planned on an all-night stay-out. They'd brought their lamps, but not enough oil for these hours and hours of waiting. So they said to the sensible ones, "Give us some of your oil, because our lamps are going out." And the wise ones answered, "No, there won't be enough for us and for you. Go instead to those who sell, and buy oil for yourselves" (Matt. 25:8–9).

The groom, of course, came while they were gone—while they were out hunting the nonexistent oil-selling shops that were open at three in the morning. But the ones who'd planned and had been responsible were able to adjust to the change in circumstances. They were ready and in the right place, even when the unpredictable happened.

Jesus had earlier given a good visual on what this difference between wisdom and foolishness looks like: "Everyone who hears these words of Mine and acts on them will be like a sensible man who built his house on the rock. The rain fell, the rivers rose, and the winds blew and pounded that house. Yet it didn't collapse, because its foundation was on the rock.

"But everyone who hears these words of Mine and doesn't act on them will be like a foolish man who built his house on the sand. The rain fell, the rivers rose, the winds blew and pounded that house, and it collapsed. And"—for emphasis here—"its collapse was great!" (Matt. 7:24–27).

If we could ask the people who were "eating, drinking, buying, selling, planting, building" (Luke 17:28), "marrying and giving in marriage" in those days before the flood, up "until the day Noah boarded the ark," they would tell us—as Jesus did—"they didn't know" they'd been acting foolishly "until the flood came and swept them all away" (Matt. 24:38–39). Didn't realize the cost of what they were putting off. Didn't realize that all their small talk and short-term interests would someday produce nothing of value, that it would bite so hard in the end. They were caught unaware . . . though God had given them warning and alerted them to what was coming.

He's done the same with us.

Our most important planning, of course—Jesus' primary meaning behind these sayings and teachings—is to be watching and waiting for His return, when all accounts will be settled and His people will be redeemed through His saving work and their trust in His blood. But one of the trickle-down takeaways of His instruction involves our wise head of planning and preparation in other matters of life. Not the least of which is wise planning with our money.

It's not just a *good* thing to do.

It's a godly thing to do.

For Family and Bible Study Discussion

1. What's your initial reaction to hearing Jesus tell us to be gravely serious about the choices and commitments we make in life? Does He leave much room for fun?

2. What makes Christians typically less financially astute as unbelievers? When is this a good thing? When is it maybe *not* such a good thing?

3. What do your financial plans look like? Feel pretty good about them?

4. What would you consider the worst potential dangers of not handling money wisely? How have you learned some of these lessons the hard way?

Words of Jesus from this chapter—Matt. 7:24–27; Matt. 10:16; Matt. 17:25–27; Matt. 24:38–39; Matt. 25:1–10; Mark 12:17; Luke 14:28–31; Luke 16:1–9; Luke 17:28

12

On Goals

Your Best Investments Are in the Kingdom

*Seek first the kingdom of God and His
righteousness, and all these things will be
provided for you. (Matthew 6:33)*

The kingdom of God is not an easy concept to understand, communicate, or internalize. If it were, someone much less smart than God would've dreamed it up. But as it is, the kingdom and Jesus' teaching on the subject carry all the vastness, power, reach, and eternity of God. In fact, if we could centralize a single theme of all He said and taught, it would surely hinge around His first words of mission: "Repent, because the kingdom of heaven has come near" (Matt. 4:17).

The kingdom of God. The kingdom of heaven. *The kingdom.* It is the sovereign reign of God. It's not a place. It's not a planet. It happens here on the earth, yes, but it happens everywhere, over everything. We as individuals carry our cards and licenses and passports and other forms of identification, marking our citizenship and homeland and places of residence.

But much broader—infinitely more extreme and limitless, immense beyond all our imagining—is a rule bigger than any White House or statehouse or even a potentially frightening one-world power collecting all nations of the earth under its control.

The kingdom of God is over all. Over us.

And definitely over the handling of our money.

It's interesting, actually, that when the Gospel writers captured some of Jesus' most compact teachings on the kingdom, He turned to financial themes to help us understand it.

"The kingdom of heaven is like treasure, buried in a field, that a man found and reburied. Then in his joy he goes out and sells everything he has and buys that field" (Matt. 13:44). It's worth everything we own, everything we possess—whatever it takes to plant our feet on it.

"Again, the kingdom of heaven is like a merchant in search of fine pearls. When he found one priceless pearl"—the one unlike any other—"he went and sold everything he had, and bought it" (vv. 45–46). The kingdom is our one thing. Above all things.

So when Jesus began traveling into the various towns and villages, He taught and healed and was "preaching the good news of the kingdom" (Matt. 9:35). He realized, of course, more than we can fathom, just how desperately these people needed what He was describing to them. That's why, seeing the crowds, "He felt compassion for them, because they were weary and worn out, like sheep without a shepherd" (v. 36). And so He turned to His disciples, and said to them, "The harvest is abundant, but the workers are few. Therefore, pray to the Lord of the harvest to send out workers into His harvest" (vv. 37–38). *Join Me on mission to introduce the kingdom of God to the world.*

And that, too, is our mission. Our goal.

With our money and with everything.

Heavenly Treasure

"Treasures in heaven." That's what Jesus said we're supposed to be collecting for ourselves on the earth. But how do we do that really? Go to church more? Read our Bible more? Be more generous and giving? Sure. There's some heavenly treasure to be found in all of that. But . . .

Heaven. What is going to be in heaven? God will be there. Angels will be there. *People* will be there. Not exactly the way we're accustomed to seeing them or interacting with them or experiencing their company. Our bodies will be new, better, different. *Incredible.* But the people of God—people who even right now are all around us—known to Him, even if not known to us . . .

Outside of God Himself, people are the only things we'll encounter today that possess an eternal quality inside them, given by God to them.

To invest in people is to deposit treasure in heaven.

That's why when Jesus first met up with Peter and Andrew, with James and John, His call to these seasoned fishermen was, "Follow Me, and I will make you fish for people" (Matt. 4:19). "From now on you will be catching people" (Luke 5:10). Immediately they "brought [their] boats to land, left everything, and followed Him" (v. 11). To be part of reaching people. To be part of helping others experience what they themselves had experienced at the quickening call of Jesus.

So while Jesus was definitely all in favor of giving one's financial gifts to God—an action we would equate to giving in church and contributing to its various ministries and outreaches—He said other important matters were involved in this act as well that could generate even greater treasures, could make them even more complete gifts.

"If you are offering your gift on the altar, and there you remember that your brother has something against you, leave your gift there in front of the altar. First go and be reconciled with your brother, and then come and offer your gift" (Matt. 5:23–24).

Imagine the impact of this statement on Jesus' original listeners. The altar was in Jerusalem. Many of the Jewish people would need to travel for days to reach it and offer their sacrifice. So if the "brother" in Jesus' example referred to someone back home, it meant packing your bags, starting out on a return trip, then locating the person you'd gotten crossways with. It turned one trip into two. Turned a clean act of responsible, sacrificial devotion into possibly a messy interaction with a neighbor, business associate, or family member. Wouldn't it be better, we'd argue, just to perform our religious duty now and get back around to talking to this guy or girl later? (If ever?) Because there would be tension in bringing it up. There would potentially be no resolution anyway. It could drag on for days and still only succeed at getting others angrier at us than before. Why does this really matter right now?

It matters because people, too, are eternal. Because relationships are spiritually valuable. Because—as John the apostle learned from Jesus—"the person who does not love his brother he has seen cannot love the God he has not seen. And we have this command from Him: The one who loves God must also love his brother" (1 John 4:20–21). To quote even more directly from Jesus: "By this all people will know that you are My disciples, if you have love for one another" (John 13:35). And probably *won't* know it by the mere fact that you paid your tithes this week, especially if you've been a bear to people on the days leading up to it. Maybe even on the ride over from home to church.

(Ouch.)

So when considering your investment goals for *all* your resources—your time, your talents, your words, your work; including, of course, how you invest your money—how many of these goals involve investing in others? As opposed to primarily yourself?

Maybe the cost of a nice lunch or dinner, in an attempt to clear the air and restore fellowship with someone whose friendship you've been missing, would be one of the best ways you could spend a few dollars this week.

It'd be a treasure in heaven.

Maybe paying for your kids' soccer cleats or guitar strings or entry fees to a summer camp—matched, of course, with the investment of your genuine interest, your involvement, and your engagement in teaching them valuable lessons for life—would qualify as a better use for an unbudgeted item this month than, say, just about anything else you've had your envious eye on.

It could come with kingdom implications.

Investing in someone you love can do that.

Jesus said the kingdom "is like a mustard seed that a man took and sowed in the field" (Matt. 13:31). It wasn't much. Didn't amount to a sizable investment. God doesn't need a lot from us to adorn it with a bountiful rate of return. The important thing wasn't the seed itself or even its miniature size. What mattered was that the seed was planted. *Invested.* Placed into the soil where something good could come from it. For over time, that seed sown in kingdom soil can grow into a tree. The tree can shoot forth its arms and branches. And then an amazing thing happens. People—as numerous as the "birds of the sky" (v. 32)—come to nest there and be attracted to its shade. The quality of our investments, blessed with the nourishment of God's care and provision, branch out in ways that touch and impact other people. Causing them to want God and be changed by His gospel. Causing them to want to honor Him with the excellence of their work and service and the development of their gifts. Causing them to know where to come when life is too hard to figure out, endure, and manage alone.

They come to someone whose goal is to invest in the kingdom of God. And these investors, praising God for giving them a humble seat at His banquet table, look around and realize they're collecting treasures in heaven already.

Real Blessings

We are born with a thirst for attainment. From the moment we recognize the shiny weight of a handful of change, or get our first crisp sample of paper money, we know we want more of that. Money, we realize, is good stuff to have. It's ice cream and soda pop and immediate plush-toy gratification from the claw machine at Walmart.

Soon, of course, it's much more. It's a new top, a pair of jeans, the latest thing in cool, casual sneakers. It's a job we hope pays more than enough, so we can *make* more than enough, so we can *buy* more than enough, so we can *be* more than enough. *Money* and *more* just naturally seem to go together.

Jesus' disciples, recognizing how poorly their financial prospects now appeared, having virtually abandoned their careers to follow Him, looked down the road and saw this innate goal of attainment slipping fast away from them. Being rich wasn't going to happen for them if they held to this current course. So Peter, as usual speaking for the group, chirped up one day and said, "Look, we have left everything and followed You. So what will there be for us?" (Matt. 19:27).

Notice first what Jesus *didn't* say. He didn't shame Peter for wondering what would become of himself and his family, financially speaking. He didn't tell him that any desire or goal for success, even material success, is a sinful nonstarter to begin with. In fact, Jesus' answer actually validates the incentivized nature of our hearts that wants to grow and achieve and, yes (if we can say it in our hushed, spiritual voices), even be rewarded for the effort. Apparently that's not something Jesus expects us to apologize for. Perhaps that's news to some of us.

But what do we *really* want to achieve? What would be the most satisfying, fulfilling, truly enriching paybacks to receive in return for what we've put in? Of all the things that might interest and attract us and seem to be the goals for all our hard work, what would actually—if we received it—just overwhelm us? Just blow us away? Make us not know if we should laugh or shout or maybe just boo-hoo with joyful, undeserving gratitude?

"I assure you," Jesus answered Peter and all the other disciples present, "when the Son of Man sits on His glorious throne, you who have followed Me will also sit on 12 thrones, judging the 12 tribes of Israel" (v. 28). Their greatness, in other words, despite the perceived sacrifice of the moment, would finally and visibly be measured only in kingdom currency. In far superior payments.

"And everyone"—extending the range of His promise to us now—"who has left houses, brothers or sisters, father or mother, children, or fields because of My name will receive 100 times more and will inherit eternal life" (v. 29).

Exponential growth is an inheritance of the believer.

So while some of our riches may consist of the green, silver, and gold variety, the thing we're really after—the yearning we noticed when our fingers first squeezed around a quarter, then held out another hand for two—is to experience blessing. And if God, our good heavenly Father, was certain that cash and cash equivalents alone were His best blessings of all, He would likely stack them up like Pringles chips in our financial pantries. But because He can give us so much more—so—much—more—He invites us to invest in places where mustard seeds can sprout into windfalls of amazing opportunity. Where patches of kingdom real estate can zoom up in value beyond what most people, looking at the same piece of property, would ever perceive. And where one certain pearl is a priceless pearl that's worth all the other jewels put together.

Say yes.

And be blessed.

For Family and Bible Study Discussion

1. How would you say the "kingdom of God" currently factors into your financial goals?
2. What would be some specific examples of things that you now would consider to be "treasures in heaven"?
3. How could you go about making deposits into those treasures in the coming weeks?
4. What are two or three of the biggest principles you've learned or seen reinforced by looking at Jesus' teachings on money? How do you intend to put these takeaways into practice?

Words of Jesus from this chapter—Matt. 4:17; Matt. 4:19; Matt. 5:23–24; Matt. 6:33; Matt. 9:37–38; Matt. 13:31–32; Matt. 13:44–46; Matt. 19:28–29; Luke 5:10–11; John 13:35

More from B&H Books

5 Minutes with God in the Car Line
978-1-4336-4570-9
$9.99

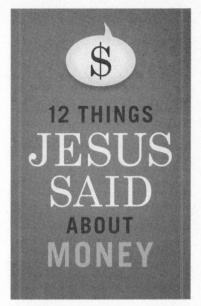

12 Things Jesus Said About Money
978-1-4336-4568-6
$9.99

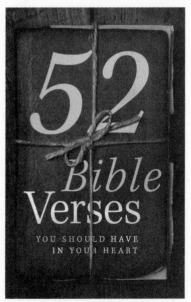

52 Bible Verses You Should
Have in Your Heart
978-1-4336-4569-3
$9.99

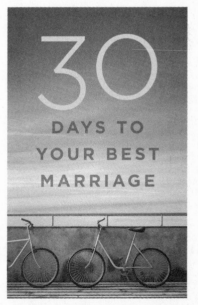

30 Days to Your Best Marriage
978-1-4336-4571-6
$9.99